CONTENTS

£17.50

Music Indexes and Bibliographies

George R. Hill, General Editor

No. 13

AN INDEX

TO EARLY MUSIC

IN SELECTED ANTHOLOGIES

by

Ruth B. Hilton

EUROPEAN AMERICAN MUSIC CORPORATION

Clifton, New Jersey

International Standard Book Number: 0-913574-13-9

PREFACE

Some years ago, the Music Library Association's Greater New York Chapter began a project to index general anthologies of music. During the next few years, considerable progress was made by several people, notably Walter Gerboth, Melva Peterson, Joseph Boonin, and Vivian Ramalingam, but the project was not completed. At the instigation of George R. Hill and the urging of Professor Gerboth, the present index was undertaken with a new plan of presentation and a revised list of indexed works.

Thanks are due all those whose aid speeded the completion of this index. I am particularly indebted to Melva Peterson, whose extensive experience with the original project proved invaluable to the early stages of this one, and who worked long hours at the start and again during the searching process. Especial gratitude is also owed Karen Famera, for her help with the initial work; Walter Parker and Victor Cardell, both of the New York University Music Library, who found answers to many questions and patiently discussed problems; George R. Hill, for editorial suggestions and oversight of production; Wiley Hitchcock, many of whose excellent ideas were incorporated, and whose perspective often prevented pitfalls; and Walter Gerboth, for his unstinting support and sympathetic advice throughout the undertaking.

In a work of this sort, some errors are certain to elude even the most careful checking, and I shall appreciate notice of any found.

R.B.H.
January 1978

INTRODUCTION

General anthologies were selected from those not limited
to music of a single era, medium, form, style, or country, and
whose contents include examples falling within the period from
antiquity to the end of the Baroque. Excluded are works falling
outside the chronological scope, and incomplete examples in the
two textbooks indexed. Although some of the volumes indexed are
no longer available, all are commonly held by music libraries.
(One obvious omission is the 46-volume <u>Anthology of music</u> ⌐<u>Das</u>
<u>Musikwerk</u>¬, excluded because its own index has recently appeared
as v.47 of the series.)

Anthological works vary greatly in quality and in the ex-
tent of scholarly apparatus. Inclusion of an anthology in this
index does not constitute a recommendation for purchase, nor
should exclusions be construed as a recommendation against.

Part 1 contains entries for composers and titles. Alphabe-
tizing is according to library practice, that is, word by word.
Obsolete spelling is retained. All initial articles are omitted
from title entries. In the anthological citations, reference is
to example numbers, or, in their absence, to page numbers.

Full information is given in each main entry; the descrip-
tion includes, as appropriate, caption title, type of work,
country of origin, date of composition or of first publication,
performing medium, polytexts, source, "school", and thematic-
catalog number. The commentary accompanying many anthologies
notes sources for examples, and in general they are not listed
here. On the other hand, information of various kinds was added
during routine verification in catalogs, dictionaries, and collec-
ted works. Recourse was also had to the thematic catalogs listed
on pp.ix-x, and references to them appear in the descriptions.

Chants and other anonymous works are entered by title or
first line of text, excepting dances, which are entered by form
(e.g., Estampie). Composer entries are, for the most part, given
as they appear in Library of Congress publications. The work

chiefly used for entries not found therein, and for emendation of dates, was <u>Die Musik in Geschichte und Gegenwart</u>. In dates, "ca." preceding the first applies to both; any other notation applies only to the date to which it is attached. The abbreviation "fl." stands for "flourished".

Uniform titles [in brackets] are those used by the Library of Congress, or are closely similar in form, so that other editions of works may be more easily found in libraries' dictionary catalogs. Many anthologies and several dictionaries also list other printed editions of works.

The notation of genre or medium indicates the subject heading under which the item falls in Part 2, where references to other works of the same kind may be found. Like the uniform titles, the subject headings are those of the Library of Congress, or are similarly formed, again to facilitate further search in a library catalog.

Added titles are given for all distinctively titled works, excerpts, captions, polytexts, and some collections; they are followed by the item numbers of main entries. In addition to serving finding purposes, these titles are helpful in locating other uses of tunes or settings of texts.

THEMATIC CATALOGS

The first column shows the abbreviation for the catalog;
the second, the composer for whom the catalog was compiled.

B. (Händel)   Bell, A. Craig.
                     Handel; chronological thematic catalogue. 2d ed.
                     Darley (England), Grian-Aig Press, 1972. 452 p.

B. (Schütz)   Bittinger, Werner.
                     Schütz-Werke-Verzeichnis (Kleine Ausgabe) Kassel,
                     Bärenreiter, 1960. 191 p.

B. (Verdelot)   Bragard, Anne Marie.
                     Étude bio-bibliographique sur Philippe Verdelot.
                     Bruxelles, Palais des Académies, 1964. (Académie
                     Royale de Belgique. Classe des beaux-arts.
                     Mémoires, ser.2, t.11, fasc.1) 197 p.

F. (WF Bach)   Falck, Martin.
                     Wilhelm Friedemann Bach; sein Leben und seine
                     Werke. Lindau, C.F. Kahnt, 1956. 166, 31p.
                         Thematic catalog appended (31 p.)

H. (Locke)   Harding, Rosamond E.M.
                     A thematic catalogue of the works of Matthew
                     Locke. Oxford (England), distributed by Black-
                     well, 1971. 177 p.

H. (Charpentier)   Hitchcock, H. Wiley.
                     The works of Marc Antoine Charpentier: catalogue
                     raisonné.
                         Forthcoming.

K. (Buxtehude)   Karstädt, Georg.
                     Thematisch-systematisches Verzeichnis der musika-
                     lischen Werke von Dietrich Buxtehude. Wiesbaden,
                     Breitkopf & Härtel, 1974. 245 p.

K. (D Scarlatti)   Kirkpatrick, Ralph.
                     Domenico Scarlatti. Princeton NJ, Princeton
                     University Press, c1973. 482 p.
                         Later printings contain corrections.
                         Contains a catalog of the sonatas and a con-
                         cordance with Longo's numbering; both appear
                         also in each volume of Kirkpatrick's edition
                         of the complete keyboard works (New York,
                         Johnson Reprint, 1972).

Thematic catalogs

K. (Fux)   Köchel, Ludwig.
                   Johann Joseph Fux, Hofcompositor... Wien,
                   Hölder, 1872. 584, 187 p. (Reprint: Hildesheim,
                   Olms, 1974)
                        Thematic catalog (Beilage X) appended (187 p.)

P. (Regnart)   Pass, Walter.
                   Thematischer Katalog sämtlicher Werke Jacob
                   Regnarts. Wien, Böhlau, 1969. 244 p. (Tabulae
                   musicae austriacae, Bd.5)

S. (JS Bach)   Schmieder, Wolfgang.
                   Thematisch-systematisches Verzeichnis der musi-
                   kalischen Werke von Johann Sebastian Bach (BWV)
                   Wiesbaden, Breitkopf & Härtel, 1966. 747 p.

W. (CPE Bach)   Wotquenne, Alfred.
                   Thematisches Verzeichnis der Werke von Carl
                   Philipp Emanuel Bach. Leipzig, Breitkopf & Härtel,
                   1905. 109 p. (Reprinted 1964)

Z. (H Purcell)   Zimmerman, Franklin B.
                   Henry Purcell, 1659-1695: an analytical catalogue
                   of his music. London, Macmillan; New York, St
                   Martin's Press, 1963. 575 p.

ANTHOLOGIES INDEXED
with citation abbreviations

Amb Ambros, August Wilhelm.
    Geschichte der Musik. 3. Aufl., hrsg. von Otto Kade.
    Leipzig, Leuckart, 1887-1911. 5 v. (Reprint: Hildesheim,
    Olms, 1968)
      Bd.5: Auserwählte Tonwerke der berühmtesten Meister des
      15. und 16. Jahrhunderts; eine Beispielsammlung zum
      dritten Bande. 605 p.

Ein Einstein, Alfred.
    A short history of music. Translated from the German.
    4th American ed., rev. New York, Knopf, 1954. 438 p.
      Musical examples, pp.257-438. Contents varies from
      that of earlier editions. Later issues are unchanged
      reprints.

Flor Florilegium musicum; history of music in 180 examples from
    antiquity to the 18th century. Selection and notes by
    Erwin Leuchter. Buenos Aires, Ricordi Americana [c1964]
    359 p. and Supplement, 75 p.

Glea Gleason, Harold, ed.
    Examples of music before 1400. [2d, corrected, printing]
    New York, Appleton-Century-Crofts [1945, c1942] 117 p.
    (Eastman School of Music series)

HAM Historical anthology of music, by Archibald T. Davison and
    Willi Apel. Cambridge, Harvard University Press.
      v.1, rev. ed., 1949 and later printings (nos.1-181)
      v.2, 1950 and later printings (nos.182-310)

Hamb Hamburg, Otto, ed.
    Musikgeschichte in Beispielen, von der Antike bis Johann
    Sebastian Bach. Wilhelmshaven, Heinrichshofen [c1976]
    239 p. (Taschenbücher zur Musikwissenschaft, 39)
      An edition containing English translation of the notes
      is scheduled to appear early 1978.

Lern Lerner, Edward R., compiler.
    Study scores of musical styles. New York, McGraw-Hill
    [c1968] 271 p.

MM Masterpieces of music before 1750; an anthology of musical
    examples from Gregorian chant to J.S. Bach. Compiled and
    edited by Carl Parrish and John F. Ohl. New York, W.W.
    Norton [c1951] 235 p.

Min   Minor, Andrew Collier, ed.
          Music in medieval and renaissance life...1200-1614.
          Columbia, University of Missouri Press [c1964] 121 p.

Nort   The Norton scores; an anthology for listening. Edited by
          Roger Kamien. Standard ed., rev. [1 v.] New York,
          W.W. Norton [c1972] 1075 p.

Nort3   ___ ___. 3d ed., expanded. 2 v. [c1977]
          v.1: Gregorian chant to Beethoven. 750 p.

OM   The Oxford anthology of music: Medieval music, edited by
          W Thomas Marrocco and Nicholas Sandon. London; New York,
          Oxford University Press [c1977] 239 p.
            A companion volume of Renaissance music is in preparation.

RMA   Reese, Gustave.
          Music in the Middle Ages. With an introduction on the music
          of ancient times. New York, W.W. Norton [c1940] 502 p.
            Only complete examples are indexed.

RR   Reese, Gustave.
          Music in the Renaissance. Rev. ed. New York, W.W. Norton
          [c1959] 1022 p.
            Only complete examples are indexed.

SS   Schirmer scores; a repertory of western music, by Joscelyn
          Godwin. New York, Schirmer Books [c1975] 1102 p.

Scher   Schering, Arnold, ed.
          Geschichte der Musik in Beispielen. Leipzig, Breitkopf &
          Härtel [1957? c1931] 481 p.
            Includes 1954 additions (nos.I-XI) ed. by Walther Vetter.

Starr   Starr, William Joseph, ed.
          Omnibus; music scores [ed. by] W.J. Starr and George F.
          Devine. Englewood Cliffs, N.J., Prentice-Hall [c1964] 2 v.
            v.1: Earliest music through the works of Beethoven. 389 p.

TEM   A Treasury of early music; an anthology of masterworks of the
          Middle Ages, the Renaissance, and the Baroque era. Compiled
          and edited by Carl Parrish. New York, W.W.Norton [c1958] 331 p.

Wolf   Wolf, Johannes.
          Sing- und Spielmusik aus älterer Zeit. Beispielband zur
          Allgemeinen Musikgeschichte. Zweite Aufl. Leipzig, Quelle &
          Meyer, 1931. 158 p.
            Reprinted as an "American edition" entitled Music of
            earlier times (New York, Broude Bros. [c1947])

Part 1: COMPOSERS and TITLES

The first column shows the item number of the main entry; the second, citations to the anthologies. Numerical references following titles are to item numbers.

A ce joly moys, 821.

A dew, my hartis lust, 373.

A Dieu commant amouretes, 16.

A l'entrant d'esté, 194.

A l'heure que je voux p.x., 411.

A la cheminee, 333.

1	Glea 12 Min 3	A l'entrade del tens clar. Troubadour ballade. 12th cent. Voice with chorus.
2	RMA 51	A la fontenele. Trouvère pastourelle.

A lieta vita, 610.

A ma damme playsant, 900.

A Madre, 40.

A Paris, 1149.

A questi suoni, 304.

3	OM 4	A summo caelo. Psalmellus from Mass for the second Sunday in Advent. Ambrosian chant.
4	HAM 21b	A tutta gente. Ballata. Lauda, 13th cent.
5	Scher 277	ABACO, Evaristo Felice dall', 1675-1742. ⌐Concerti à più istrumenti, op.6. No.11. Aria canta- bile⌐ 2d movement. Violin with string orchestra.
6	HAM 269	⌐Sonate da chiesa e da camera à tre, violins & continuo, op.3. No.2. Allegro⌐ 2d movement. Trio-sonata.
7	Scher 204	ABBATINI, Antonio Maria, 1597(ca.)-1679? ⌐Dal male il bene. E che farete amanti⌐ Voice with instrumental ensemble.

Abraham, 284.

Accessit ad pedes Jesu, 979.

Acceso, 611.

Ach Golgatha, 120.

Ach, Herr, lass dein lieb' Engelein, 114.

Ach, Herr, mich armen Sünder, 1158.

Ach lieb mit leid, 774.

Ach schatz ich thu dir klagen, 757.

Ach, süsse Seel', 755.

Achetez à ma boutique, 1239.

Acquaint thyself with God, 674.

Actes of the Apostles, 1539.

Ad coenam agni providi, 312.

8   RMA 118   Ad mortem festinamus.
     Dance of death. Song. Spanish, 14th cent. 1 voice.

9   Glea 10   ADAM de la Halle, ca.1235-1288.
     HAM 36c   [Diex soit] Ballade. 3 voices.

10   Glea 74   [Fines amouretes] Virelai. 3 voices.

11   Scher 14   [Hélas! il n'est mais] Trouvère song.

12   Glea 16   [Le jeu de Robin et de Marion] Trouvère dramatic
     pastoral.

13   Hamb 8   [Le jeu de Robin et de Marion. Bergeronnete] Trouvère.
     2 solo voices.

14   RMA 53   [Le jeu de Robin et de Marion. Robins m'aime]
     Trouvère rondeau.

15   HAM 36a   [Li maus d'amer] Trouvère ballade.

16   Glea 76   [Rondeaux, 3 part. A Dieu commant amouretes]

17   OM 56   [Rondeaux, 3 part. Hé Diex! quant verrai]

18   HAM 36b   [Rondeaux, 3 part. Tant con je vivrai]

19   HAM 16c   ADAM de Saint-Victor, d.1192.
     [Jubilemus salvatori] Rhymed sequence.

Adelaide, 1361.

Adieu m'amour et ma maistresse, 184.

Adieu mes amours, 412.

Adjuro vos, 1169.

Adonis, 846.

Adonis Tod, 858.

Adoramus te, Christe, 907.

Aeide musa moi phile, 1020.

20   HAM 9b   Aeterna Christi munera.
     Ambrosian hymn. 2 versions, 9th cent. and the presumed
     original.

21   SS 3a   Aeterna Christi munera.
     Gregorian hymn. Words 5th cent. (by St. Ambrose?).

Aeterna Christi munera, 20, 21, 1174.

22   HAM 9a   Aeterne rerum conditor.
     RMA 18   Hymn. Ambrosian chant. 3 versions, 12th-14th cent.

Afferte gladium, 297.

Affetti musicali, 995-996.

Agincourt, Perrin d'. see PERRIN d'Agincourt

23 Flor 32a   Agnus Dei.
   SS 6a   Gregorian chant, 13th cent. From Mass Ordinary XVII.

24 MM 7   Agnus Dei.
           Trope in free organum, 12th cent. 2 voices.

Agnus Dei, 23, 24, 185.

25 Scher 227 AGOSTINI, Pietro Simone, 1640(ca.)-1680.
          ⌐Il ratto delle Sabine. Se tu non m'ami⌐ Canzonette.
          Voice with instrumental ensemble.

26 Amb 57c   AGRICOLA, Alexander, 1446-1506.
          ⌐Amor, che sospirar⌐ Frottola. 3 voices. Without
          text. Incomplete.

27 Scher 53   ⌐Belle sur toutes⌐ Polyphonic chanson. 3 voices.
          Polytext: Belle sur toutes; Tota pulchra es.

28 Amb 23   ⌐Comme femme, 3 voices⌐ Chanson.

29 Wolf 17   ⌐Oublier veul⌐ Polyphonic chanson. 3 voices. Without
          text.

Ah Belinda, 1274.

Ah ma soeur, 274.

Ah quanto è vero, 324.

30 HAM 166   AICHINGER, Gregor, 1564-1628.
          ⌐Factus est⌐ Motet. 4 voices.

Ainsi qu'on oit le cerf bruire, 667.

Al suon, 73.

Al valor del mio brando, 730.

31 HAM 205   ALBERT, Heinrich, 1604-1651.
          ⌐Auf, mein Geist⌐ Sacred aria with instrumental ritor-
          nello.

32 Scher 193a ⌐Freundschaft⌐ Voice and continuo. Arien oder Melo-
          deyen... II, no.10.

33 Scher 193b ⌐Gespräch einer Jungfrauen⌐ 2 solo voices with contin-
          uo. Arien oder Melodeyen... I, no.6.

34 Flor 128a ⌐Die Lust hat mich gezwungen⌐ Voice and continuo.

35 Flor 128b ⌐Soll, denn, schönste Doris⌐ Voice and continuo.

36 Scher 193c ⌐Vorjahrslied⌐ 2 solo voices with continuo. Arien
          oder Melodeyen... IV, no.14.

37 Glea 34   ALBERTUS Parisiensis Magister, 12th cent.
   RMA 71   ⌐Congaudeant catholici⌐ Organum. Strophic hymn.
          Trope. ca.1140. 3 voices. Compostela school.

| 38 | Scher 214 | ALBRICI, Vincenzo, 1631-1696.
⌐Sonata, 2 violins, 2 trumpets & continuo⌐ Festliche sonate. |

Alceste, 961-963.

| 39 | Amb 57b | ALESSANDRO da Firenze, 15th cent.
⌐Teco, signora mia⌐ Frottola. 4 voices. Without text.
(Title supplied from Anthology of music, v.3, p.16) |

Alessandro severo, 960.

Alexanderfest, 720.

Alfonsina, 634.

40	HAM 22a	ALFONSO X, el Sabio, King of Castile and Leon, 1221-1284. ⌐Las cantigas de Santa Maria. A Madre⌐ Villancico. 1 voice.
41	Glea 22	⌐Las cantigas de Santa Maria. Allegria!⌐ Zajal (virelai) 1 voice.
42	HAM 22c	⌐Las cantigas de Santa Maria. Aque serven⌐ Villancico. 1 voice.
43	TEM 7	⌐Las cantigas de Santa Maria. Gran dereit'⌐ 1 voice.
44	HAM 22b	⌐Las cantigas de Santa Maria. Mais nos faz⌐ Villancico. 1 voice.
45	OM 29	⌐Las cantigas de Santa Maria. Maldito seja quen non loará⌐ Villancico. 1 voice.
46	OM 28	⌐Las cantigas de Santa Maria. Nas mentes senpre tẽer⌐ 1 voice.
47	Lern 18	⌐Las cantigas de Santa Maria. Quen Jesucrist' essa Madre⌐ Virelai. 1 voice.
48	Flor 18 RMA 65	⌐Las cantigas de Santa Maria. Rosa das rosas⌐ Virelai. 1 voice.

All Lust und Freud, 753.

Alla riva del Tebro, 1170.

| 49 | Glea 67
HAM 33a | Alle, psallite.
Motet. 13th cent. 3 voices. Polytext: Alle, psallite;
Alle, psallite; Alleluya. |

Allegria, 41.

50	Flor 4	Alleluia. Ambrosian chant, ca.4th cent.
51	Ein 4	Alleluia. Gregorian chant.
52	Flor 11	Alleluia. Gregorian chant, with sequence.

Alleluia, 49-62, 1066.

| 53 | HAM 13 | Alleluia, Angelus Domini.
Gregorian chant. |

54 Glea 28   Alleluia, Angelus Domini.
    HAM 26c   Organum. French, 11th cent. 2 voices.

55 Lern 7   Alleluia, Dominus dixit.
                   Gregorian chant, probably before 700.

56 SS 1a   Alleluia, Dulce lignum.
                   Gregorian chant. From the Mass Proper for May 3.

57 SS 1b   Alleluia, Dulce lignum.
                   Organum duplum. ca.1150-1200. Incomplete. Notre Dame
                   school.

58 OM 39   Alleluia, Justus ut palma.
                   Free organum. 2 solo voices and choir. From Ad organ-
                   um faciendum, ca.1100.

59 OM 43   Alleluia, Non vos relinquam.
                   Organum duplum. ca.1170. Notre Dame school.

60 HAM 57a   Alleluia, Psallat.
                   Motet. 14th cent. 3 voices. Worcester school.

61 Lern 23   Alleluia, Resurgens.
                   Gregorian chant.

62 OM 38   Alleluia, Te martyrum.
                   Free organum. From the Winchester Troper, ca.1050.
                   2 voices.

63 SS 9a   Allemande.
                   Monsiers almaine. English, 16th cent. 3 instruments.
                   From T. Morley's Consort lessons of 1599. Possibly by
                   William Byrd.

             Allemande 'S medelÿn, 1231.

             Alles was ihr tut, 233.

             Allon, gay Bergeres, 376.

             Allons danser, 1341.

             Alma mia, 323.

             Alma mia piange, 886.

             Alma redemptoris mater, 462-463, 483, 765, 1070, 1259.

             Alouette, 822.

64 OM 59   Alpha vibrans monumentum.
                   Isorhythmic motet. French, ca.1390. 4 voices. Poly-
                   text: Alpha vibrans; Coetus venit heroicus; Amicum
                   quaerit; textless contratenor.

             Als ick riep met verlanghen, 347.

             Als nun Jesus wusste alles, 930.

             Alta, 1518.

             Amans ames, 360.

             Amarilli mia bella, 262, 1234.

Amarotus da Caserta.   see ANTONELLO da Caserta

65 Glea 2 AMBROSIUS, Saint, Bishop of Milan, ca.340-397.
⌜Veni redemptor gentium⌝ Hymn. 1 voice.

66 RMA 52 Amereis mi vous, cuers dous?
Trouvère rondeau.

Amfiparnaso, 1545-1548.

Amicum quaerit, 64.

Amiga tengo, 506.

Amis, dolens, 706.

67 Scher 135 AMMERBACH, Elias Nikolaus, 1530(ca.)-1597.
⌜Die Megdlein sind von Flandern⌝ Dance. Keyboard.

68 HAM 154a ⌜Passamezzo, harpsichord⌝ Dance variations.   From Or-
gel oder Instrument Tabulatur, 1571.

Amor c'al tuo suggetto, 887.

Amor, che sospirar, 26.

69 OM 74 Amor mi fa cantar.
Ballata. Italian, early 14th cent. 1 voice.

Amor tu sei, 985.

Amour de moy, 902.

Amour nous traicte, 229.

Amour saltimbanque, 280.

Amours, cent mille, 829.

70 RMA 94 Amours et ma dame aussi.
Rondeau. 13th cent. 3 voices.

An den Schlaf, 659.

71 Wolf 20 ANA, Francesco d', d.1503.
⌜La luce de questi occhi⌝ Frottola. 4 voices.

72 Amb 57g ⌜Nasce l'aspro⌝ Frottola. 4 voices.

73 HAM 160 ANERIO, Felice, 1560-1614.
⌜Al suon⌝ 3 versions: 3-part song; harpsichord; lute.

74 Scher 181 ANERIO, Giovanni Francesco, 1567-1630.
⌜Gagliard⌝ 2 versions, for keyboard and for lute.

Angelica biltà, 888.

75 Glea 51 Angelus ad virginem.
Song. English, late 14th cent. Fauxbourdon style.
3 voices.

76 HAM 232 ANGLEBERT, Jean Henri d', 1628-1691.
⌜Pièces de clavecin. Suite, G minor. Selections⌝
Prélude, Allemande, Sarabande.

Anima mea, 1255.

77	Scher 120	ANIMUCCIA, Giovanni, 1500(ca.)-1571. ⌐Ben venga, amore⌐ Lauda. 4 voices.
78	Flor 68a	⌐Benedetto sia lo giorno⌐ Lauda. 4 voices.

Anmuthige Clavier-Übung, 863-864.

Annuntiantes, 1224.

Anthonello de Caserta. see ANTONELLO da Caserta

| 79 | TEM 17 | ANTONELLO da Caserta, 15th cent.
⌐Notes pour moi⌐ Polyphonic ballade. 4 voices. |
| 80 | Scher 30 | ANTONIO Romano, fl.1414.
⌐Stirps Mocenigo⌐ Motet. 2 voices and 4 brasses.
Polytext: Stirps Mocenigo; Ducalis sedes. |

Ape, the monkey, and the baboon, 1610.

Apparatus musico-organisticus, 1075.

Apparuit gratia Dei, 291.

Aptatur, 1270.

Aque serven, 42.

| 81 | Scher 94 | AQUILA, Marco d', 16th cent.
⌐Fantasia, lute⌐ |

Aquila altera, 815-816.

82	Lern 47 Nort3 9	ARCADELT, Jacob, 1505(ca.)-1568. ⌐Bianco e dolce cigno⌐ Madrigal. 4 voices.
83	Starr 36	⌐Quand je vous ayme ardentement⌐ Chanson. 4 voices.
84	Flor 80	⌐Se per colpa del vostro fiero sdegno⌐ Madrigal. 4 voices.
85	Scher 100	⌐Voi mi ponest' in foco⌐ Madrigal. 3 voices. From his Madrigals, book 1 (1542).
86	HAM 130	⌐Voi ve n'andat' al cielo⌐ Madrigal. 4 voices.

Arde il mio petto, 263.

Argia, 323.

Aria allemagna, 1246.

Aria della battaglia, 1167.

Ariadne musica, 543-544.

Armide, 964-966.

| 87 | HAM 290 | ARNE, Thomas Augustine, 1710-1778.
⌐The fall of Phaeton. Come my dearest⌐ Song with in-
strumental ensemble. |

Arnold de Lantins. see LANTINS, Arnold de

As Vesta was descending, 1611.

Ascanio, Jusquin d'. see DEPRÈS, Josquin

Ascendo ad patrem, 1175.

88 Flor 6   Asperges me, Domine.
               Gregorian chant. 13th cent. Antiphon, with Psalm 50
               (51): Miserere mei, Deus.

            Astianatte, 201.

89 Wolf 24   ASTON, Hugh, probably 1480-1522.
               [Hornpipe, virginals] Variations, in part.

            Atressi com l'olifanz, 1326.

90 OM 22   Au renouvel du tens.
               Trouvère pastourelle, lai form. 13th cent.

            Aucun ont trouvé, 1224.

            Audivi vocem, 1481.

            Auf, mein Geist, 31.

            Augoustou monarkhesantos, 838.

            Auguste, 379.

            Aures ad nostras deitatis, 464.

91 Scher 44 Aus fahr ich hin.
               Song. German, ca.1460. 3 voices.

            Aus tiefer Not, 216, 855, 945, 1593.

92 Wolf 36   Auss guetem Grund.
               Minnelied auf Isabella. 16th cent. 4 voices.

93 OM 18   Autrier m'iere levaz.
               Troubadour pastourelle, late 12th cent.

            Autr'ier tout seus, 1325.

            Autumno, 1583.

94 TEM 10   Ave gloriosa mater.
               Motet. 13th cent. 3 voices. Polytext: Ave, virgo;
               Ave gloriosa mater; Domino.

95 Glea 2   Ave Maria.
               Ambrosian chant. 12th cent.

            Ave Maria coelorum, 474.

            Ave Maria gratia plena, 413, 547, 1153.

            Ave maris stella, 254, 313, 465, 484.

            Ave mater Domini, 1147.

96 Scher 51 Ave mitis, ave pia.
               Lauda. ca.1460. 3 voices.

            Ave regina coelorum, 334, 579, 661, 1120.

            Ave rosa sine spinnis, 1430.

            Ave sanctissima, 1556.

            Ave, virgo, 94.

97	Scher 301	BACH, Carl Philipp Emanuel, 1714-1788. ⌐Geistliche Oden und Lieder, W.194 ⌐no. 27⌐ Preis des Schöpfers⌐ Wenn ich, O Schöpfer, deine Macht. With harpsichord.
98	Scher 304	⌐Musikalisches Allerley, 2. Sammlung. Les langueurs tendres⌐ Harpsichord. W.117 ⌐no.30⌐
99	HAM 296	⌐Musikalisches Vielerley. Fantasia, G minor⌐ Harpsichord. W.117 ⌐no.13⌐
100	Scher 303	⌐Sonata, harpsichord, W.48, no.1, F major. Allegro⌐ 1st movement.
101	SS 57	⌐Sonata, harpsichord, W.49, no.3, E minor⌐
102	HAM 297	⌐Sonata, harpsichord, W.55, no.3. Cantabile⌐ 2d movement. From his Clavier-Sonaten für Kenner und Liebhaber, 1. Sammlung.
103	Flor 174	⌐Sonata, harpsichord, W.55, no.5. Adagio maestoso⌐ 2d movement. From his Clavier-Sonaten für Kenner und Liebhaber, 1. Sammlung.
104	HAM 303	BACH, Johann Christian, 1735-1782. ⌐Sonata, piano, op.17, no.4, G major. Allegro⌐ First movement.
105	HAM 237	BACH, Johann Christoph, 1642-1703. ⌐Prelude and fugue, organ, E-flat major⌐
		BACH, Johann Sebastian, 1685-1750. Brandenburg concertos. see his ⌐Concerti grossi⌐
106	MM 48	⌐Christ lag in Todesbanden, S.4. Es war ein wunderlicher Krieg⌐ No.5 of the cantata. Chorus. 4th stanza of text.
107	MM 46	⌐Christ lag in Todesbanden, S.4. Wir essen und leben wohl⌐ No.8 of the cantata. Final chorale. 7th stanza of text; 1st stanza underlaid.
108	Nort 10 Nort3 24 Starr 126	⌐Concerto grosso, no.2, F major⌐ Brandenburg concerto. S.1047.
109	Starr 152	⌐Ein' feste Burg ist unser Gott, S.80⌐ Cantata.
110	Starr 149	⌐Ein' feste Burg ist unser Gott, S.720⌐ Chorale prelude.
111	Nort 9 Nort3 23	⌐Fugue, organ, S.578, G minor⌐
112	Scher 284	⌐Ich bin ein guter Hirt, S.85. Seht, was die Liebe tut⌐ No.5 of the cantata. Tenor aria.
113	Lern 86	⌐Jesu, der du meine Seele, S.78⌐ Cantata.
114	Scher 285	⌐Johannespassion, S.245. Ach Herr, lass dein lieb' Engelein⌐ Final chorale.
115	MM 50	⌐Die Kunst der Fuge. Contrapunctus 3⌐ Fugue. 4 instruments. S.1080, no.3.

116 Nort 14   ⌐Mass, S.232, B minor. Crucifixus⌐ Chorus with piano reduction of the orchestral accompaniment.

117 SS 45   ⌐Mass, S.232, B minor. Sanctus⌐ Chorus and orchestra.

118 Hamb 60b   ⌐Matthäuspassion, S.244. No.63⌐ O Haupt voll Blut und Wunden. Chorale. 4 voices.

119 Starr 117   ⌐Matthäuspassion, S.244. No.68-73⌐ Recitatives and aria (Sehet, Jesus hat die Hand) with chorus, and chorale (Wenn ich einmal soll scheiden).

120 MM 49   ⌐Matthäuspassion, S.244. No.69⌐ Ach Golgatha. Alto recitative.

121 Flor 162   ⌐Musikalisches Opfer. Selections⌐ S.1079, no.3a (Canones diversi; Canon a 2) and 3c (a 2; Per motum contrarium ⌐3 instruments⌐).

122 Scher 286   ⌐Notenbuch der Anna Magdalena Bach (1725) Willst du dein Herz mir schenken⌐ Song, with harpsichord. S.518 (no.37 of the Notenbuch).

123 Lern 85   ⌐Nun komm, der Heiden Heiland, S.659⌐ Chorale prelude.

124 Flor 163   ⌐O Ewigkeit, du Donnerwort, S.60. Es ist genug⌐ No.5 of the cantata. Final chorale.

125 MM 47   ⌐Orgelbüchlein. Christ lag in Todesbanden⌐ Chorale prelude. S.625.

126 Starr 149   ⌐Oreglbüchlein. Durch Adams Fall ist ganz verderbt⌐ Chorale prelude. S.637.

127 Hamb 92c   ⌐Orgelbüchlein. Gelobet seist du, Jesu Christ⌐ Chorale prelude. S.604.

128 Starr 148   ⌐Orgelbüchlein. In dulci jubilo⌐ Chorale prelude. S.608.

129 HAM 190d   ⌐Orgelbüchlein. Vater unser im Himmelreich⌐ Chorale prelude. S.636.

130 Starr 151   ⌐Orgelbüchlein. Wenn wir in höchsten Nöthen sein⌐ Chorale prelude. S.641.

131 Starr 138   ⌐Partita, harpsichord, S.828, D major⌐ No.4.

132 SS 39   ⌐Passacaglia, organ, S.582, C minor⌐ Passacaglia and fugue.

133 Scher 283   ⌐Prelude and fugue, organ, S.542, G minor⌐

134 Ein 33   ⌐Suite, harpsichord, S.808, G minor. Prelude⌐ From English suite no.3.

135 SS 11   ⌐Suite, harpsichord, S.817, E major⌐ French suite no.6.

136 Nort 11
Nort3 25   ⌐Suite, orchestra, S.1068, D major. Selections⌐ Air and Gigue from suite no.3.

137 Starr 151   ⌐Vor deinen Thron tret' ich, S.668⌐ Chorale prelude.

138 Nort 13
Nort3 26   ⌐Wachet auf, ruft uns die Stimme, S.140⌐ Cantata.

139 Starr 182   ⌐Das wohltemperierte Clavier. Th.1, no.1⌐ Prelude and
                     fugue in C major. S.846.

140 Nort 12   ⌐Das wohltemperierte Clavier. Th.1, no.2⌐ Prelude and
     Starr 184   fugue in C minor. S.847.

141 Lern 84   ⌐Das wohltemperierte Clavier. Th.1, no.6. Fugue⌐
                     G minor. S.851.

142 Starr 186   ⌐Das wohltemperierte Clavier. Th.1, no.8⌐ Prelude and
                     fugue in E-flat minor. S.853.

143 Flor 171   BACH, Wilhelm Friedemann, 1710-1784.
                     ⌐Fantasia, piano, F.20, E minor⌐

144 HAM 289   ⌐Fugues, harpsichord, F.31. D minor⌐ Fugue no.4 of
                     his Fugen und Polonaisen.

145 HAM 288   ⌐Polonaises, harpsichord, F.12. C minor⌐ No.2 of his
                     12 Polonaisen.

                     Baisiez moy, 414.

                     Bald die Blonde, 770.

                     Balen, 1460.

                     Ballet du Roy, 1266.

146 Scher 237   BALTZAR, Thomas, 1630(ca.)-1663.
                     ⌐Allemande, violin, C minor⌐

                     Banchetto musicale, 1393-1394.

147 Flor 111   BANCHIERI, Adriano, 1567-1634.
                     ⌐Fantasia⌐ 4 instruments.

148 Flor 110   ⌐La pazzia senile. Burattin estu ti⌐ 3 voices.

149 Scher 151   ⌐Sinfonia d'istromenti senza voci⌐ 4 instruments.
                     No.13 of his Ecclesiastiche sinfonie (1607).

150 HAM 186   ⌐Zabaione musicale⌐ Madrigal comedy. 5 voices.

151 Scher 49   BARBIREAU, Jakob, d.1491.
                     ⌐Der pfoben Swancz, 4 instruments⌐ Dance.

                     Barcelona mass. see Mass of Barcelona

                     Bartholomeus. see BARTOLOMEO

152 Min 90   BARTLET, John, fl.1606-1610.
                     ⌐A book of airs. Of all the birds that I do know⌐
                     4 voices.

153. Min 86   ⌐A book of airs. A pretty ducke there was⌐ 4 voices.

154 Amb 57a   BARTOLOMEO, 15th cent.
                     ⌐Si talor quella⌐ Frottola. 3 voices.

155 Flor 82a   Basse danse.
                     Cueur angiosseux. French, ca.1530. Lute.

156 Lern 46   Basse danse.
                     Patience. Lute. (Attaingnant, 1529).

157 Scher 90   Basse danse.
                     Sans roch. Lute. (Attaingnant, 1529).

Bataille, 1472.

158 SS 9b BATCHELAR, Daniell.
  ⌐Monsiers almaine⌐ Lute. From Robert Dowland's Vari-
  etie of lute lessons, 1610.

159 Min 101 Battle calls.
  For renaissance trumpet. 16th cent.

Be m'an perdut, 173-174.

Beata Dei genitrix, 401.

Beata progenies, 1256.

160 OM 55 Beata viscera.
  Conductus-motet. English, late 13th cent. 3 voices.

161 Flor 42 Beata viscera.
  Fauxbourdon. 14th cent. 3 voices. Incomplete.

Beata viscera, 160-161, 1214.

162 OM 6 Beatus vir.
  Psalm, with antiphon Erat autem aspectus. 3d psalm at
  Vespers on Easter day. Gregorian chant, 8th psalm tone.

163 Scher 217 Beau berger Tirsis (Brunette)
  French, 1661. Voice with instrumental bass.

164 OM 93 BEDINGHAM, Johannes, 15th cent.
  ⌐Missa, Dueil angoisseus. Credo⌐ 3 voices.

Bedyngham, John. see BEDINGHAM, Johannes

Beggar's opera, 1195-1198.

Behold thou hast made my days, 636.

Belle bonne, sage, 361.

Belle Hermione, 967.

Belle sur toutes, 27.

Belle, veuillies moy retenir, 466.

Bells, 243.

Ben nochier costante, 1208.

Ben venga, amore, 77.

Benche amor mi faccia, 1524.

165 Wolf 33 BENDUSI, Francesco.
  ⌐Opera nova de balli. Speranza⌐ Ballo. 4 instruments. Published 1553.

Benedetto sia lo giorno, 78.

166 HAM 28d-e Benedicamus Domino.
  Hamb 20   Clausulae. ca.1200. 2 voices. Notre Dame school.

167 HAM 28a Benedicamus Domino.
  Hamb 18   Gregorian chant.

168	HAM 28b	Benedicamus Domino. 　Organum. ca.1125. 2 voices. Compostela school.
169	HAM 28c	Benedicamus Domino. 　Organum. ca.1175. 2 voices. Notre Dame school.
170	Glea 30 MM 8 Starr 15	Benedicamus Domino. 　Organum. Opening of the trope. Early 12th cent. 　2 voices. St. Martial school.

Benedicamus Domino, 166-170, 1321, 1465.

Benedicamus Dominus, 525.

171	OM 88	BENET, Joannes, 15th cent. 　⌐Telus purpurium⌐ Isorhythmic motet. 3 voices. Poly- 　text: Telus purpurium; Splendida flamigero; textless 　tenor.
172	MM 28	BENNET, John, fl.1570-1615. 　⌐Madrigals (1599) Thyrsis, sleepest thou?⌐ 4 voices.

Berbigant. see BARBIREAU, Jakob

Bergeronnete, 13.

Bernardina, 415, 1450.

173	HAM 18b	BERNART de Ventadorn, 12th cent. 　⌐Be m'an perdut⌐ Troubadour canso.
174	Glea 15 TEM 6	⌐Be m'an perdut⌐ Troubadour song. 　(Not the same as HAM 18b)
175	Glea 15 OM 14	⌐Can vei la lauzeta⌐ Troubadour vers.
176	Lern 12	⌐Lancan vei la folha⌐ Troubadour song.
177	Glea 14 RMA 49	⌐Pois preyatz me, senhor⌐ Troubadour canso.
178	Glea 20	⌐Pois preyatz me, senhor; arr.⌐ Deich von der guoten 　schiet. Minnelied: German text by Friedrich von Hüsen 　set to Bernart's tune (see 177).
179	Scher 213b	BERNHARD, Christoph, 1627-1692. 　⌐Herr, nun lässest du deinen Diener. Sonata⌐ Over- 　ture. 2 violins, 2 violas, bassoon and organ.

Bianco e dolce cigno, 82.

Biauté parée de valour, 710.

BIBER, Heinrich Ignaz Franz von, 1644-1704.
　Mystery sonatas. see his ⌐Sonatas, violin & continuo
　(Bayerische Staatsbibliothek: Mus.ms.4123)⌐

180	Flor 137	⌐Sonatas, violin & continuo (Bayerische Staatsbiblio- 　thek: Mus.ms.4123) No.3, Christi Geburt. 1st move- 　ment⌐
181	Scher 238	⌐Sonatas, violin & continuo (Bayerische Staatsbiblio- 　thek: Mus.ms.4123) No.6⌐ Christi gebet auf dem Ölberg.
182	Lern 75	⌐Sonatas, violin & continuo (Bayerische Staatsbiblio- 　thek: Mus.mus.4123) No.10⌐ Die Kreuzigung Christi.

183 HAM 238   ⌈Sonatas, violin & continuo (Bayerische Staatsbiblio-thek: Mus.ms.4123) No.11⌉ Surrexit Christus hodie. Passacaglia.

Biblische Historien, 871-872.

184 MM 16   BINCHOIS, Gilles, 1400(ca.)-1460.
⌈Adieu m'amour et ma maistresse⌉ Polyphonic chanson. 3 voices.

185 Ein 12   ⌈Agnus Dei⌉ Isolated mass movement. 3 voices.

186 HAM 69   ⌈De plus en plus⌉ Rondeau. 3 voices.
    Scher 42
    SS 21

187 OM 100   ⌈Dueil angoisseus⌉ Ballade. 3 voices.

188 HAM 70   ⌈Files à marier⌉ Polyphonic chanson. 4 voices.

189 Scher 43   ⌈Magnificat, secundi toni⌉ 3 voices.

190 RR 23   ⌈Margarite, fleur de valeur⌉ Rondeau. 3 voices.

191 Flor 45   ⌈Triste plaisir⌉ Rondeau. Voice and 2 instrumental lines.

192 Wolf 13   ⌈Ut queant laxis⌉ Hymn. Fauxbourdon. 2 voices.

193 OM 95   ⌈Veni creator spiritus⌉ Hymn. Fauxbourdon. 3 voices. Original plainsong included.

Bist du der Hensel Schütze, 946.

194 Glea 14   BLONDEL de Nesle, 12th cent.
⌈A l'entrant d'esté⌉ Trouvère lai segment.

195 TEM 43   BLOW, John, 1649-1708.
⌈Service, G major. Jubilate Deo⌉ Canticle (anthem) 4 voices.

196 HAM 243   ⌈Venus and Adonis. Mourn for thy servant⌉ Chorus. 4 voices.

197 Scher 163   BODENSCHATZ, Erhard, 1576-1636.
⌈Sanguis Jesu⌉ Bicinium de Passione. 2 voices.

198 Scher 254   BÖHM, Georg, 1661-1733.
⌈Der Herr hat seinen Engeln⌉ Soprano and continuo.

199 Flor 149   ⌈Herr, wie Du willst, organ. Part 1⌉ Partita (chorale prelude) Includes the original chorale.

200 Scher 253   ⌈Suite, harpsichord, F minor. Allemande⌉

Bóg wieczny, 717.

Bon jour, bon mois, 467.

Bon jour, mon coeur, 908, 1235.

Bon vin doit, 529.

201 HAM 262   BONOCINI, Giovanni, 1670-1747.
⌈Astianatte. Deh lascia, o core⌉ Aria, with continuo.

202 Flor 150   ⌈Il Giosuè. Sommo Dio⌉ Aria, with continuo.

203 Scher 219   BONONCINI, Giovanni Maria, 1642-1678.
     ⌐Varii fiori del giardino musicale. Canone a 12 voci
     all' unisono┐ Instruments.

     Bonté bialté, 322.

     Bonzorno madonna, 1362.

204 Scher 95   BORRONO, Pietro Paolo, 16th cent.
     ⌐Saltarello chiamata La torcia┐ Lute.

205 Scher 72   BOSSINENSIS, Franciscus, fl.1509-1511.
     ⌐Non è tempo d'aspettare┐ Voice and lute. Arranged
     from the frottola of Marco Cara (see 286).

206 RR 33b   ⌐Oimè il cor┐ Frottola. Voice and lute. With its
     ricercare.

207 RR 80   BOURGEOIS, Louis, 1510-1561.
     ⌐Or sus, serviteurs du Seigneur┐ Psalm 134 (133)
     1 voice.

208 HAM 132   ⌐Qui au conseil┐ Psalm 1. 4 voices.

209 Scher 256   BOUSSET, Jean Baptiste, 1662(ca.)-1725.
     ⌐Charmante nuit┐ Air sérieux. Voice with continuo.

210 Scher 288   BOUVARD, François, 1683-1760.
     ⌐Combat des éléments┐ Song. Bass voice.

211 Scher 156   BRADE, William, 1560?-1630.
     ⌐Newe ausserlesene Paduanen, Galliarden, Cantzonen, All-
     mand und Coranten. Allemande, G major┐ 5 instruments.

     Brandenburg concerti. see BACH, JS ⌐Concerti grossi┐

212 Flor 82b   Branle gay.
     Dance. French, 16th cent. Harpsichord.

     Bransle d'ecosse, 1231.

     Bransle simple de Novelle, 1267.

213 Scher 70   BROCCO, Giovanni, 15th-16th cent.
     ⌐Ite caldi sospiri┐ Frottola. Voice and 3 instruments.

214 Wolf 23   ⌐Mai piu sera lo core┐ Frottola. 3 voices.

     Brochus, Joannes. see BROCCO, Giovanni

     Brocus, Jo. see BROCCO, Giovanni

     Browning fantasia, 245.

215 RR 201   Browning Madame.
     Canon. ca.1600. 3 voices.

216 HAM 111b   BRUCK, Arnold von, 1470(ca.)-1554.
     ⌐Aus tiefer Not┐ Chorale. 4 voices.

217 Amb 45   ⌐Es get gen disem summer┐ Lied. 4 voices.

218 Scher 110   ⌐Komm', heiliger Geist┐ Canonic motet. 4 voices.

219 Amb 44b   ⌐O allmächtiger Gott┐ Motet. 5 voices.

220 Amb 44a   ⌐O du armer Judas┐ Motet. 6 voices.

221	Amb 21	BRUMEL, Antoine, ca.1480-1520. [Missa festivale. Selections] 9 sections. 2-4 voices.
222	Scher 64	[Missa super Dringhs. Benedictus] Bicinium for organ or 2 instruments.
223	Amb 22	[Regina coeli] Motet. 4 voices.

Brunette, 163, 1528.

224	Lern 20	Bryd one brere. English song, 12th cent. 1 voice.
225	Scher 83	BUCHNER, Johann, b.1483. [Quem terra, pontus] Chorale prelude.
226	TEM 30	BULL, John, 1562 or 3-1628. [Pavane, virginals] No.12 in Parthenia...
227	HAM 178	[Praeludium, virginals] Fitzwilliam virginal book, v.1, p.158.
228	Scher 147	[Spanish paven, virginals] Variations. Fitzwilliam virginal book, v.2, p.131.

Buona figliuola, 1238.

Burattin estu ti, 148.

Buscha, 939.

229	Nort3 5	BUSNOIS, Antoine, d.1492. [Amour nous traicte] 4 voices. Polytext: Amour nous traicte; Je m'en vois.
230	Flor 55	Buxheimer Orgelbuch (15th cent.) Prelude on F.
231	HAM 84c-d Hamb 44	Buxheimer Orgelbuch (15th cent.) Preludes on G and C.
232	Scher 36	Buxheimer Orgelbuch (15th cent.) Puisque m'amour. Canzona.
233	Hamb 94	BUXTEHUDE, Dietrich, 1637-1707. [Alles was ihr tut, K.4. Alles was ihr tut] 4-part chorus from the cantata, with strings and continuo.
234	Flor 136	[Christ unser Herr zum Jordan kam, K.180] Chorale prelude. Includes the original chorale tune.
235	HAM 235	[Eins bitte ich vom Herrn, K.24. Liebster Herr Jesu] Aria and chorus with orchestra, from the cantata.
236	Hamb 92b	[Gelobet seiest du, Jesu Christ, K.189] Chorale prelude.
237	Starr 104	[In dulci jubilo, K.197] Chorale prelude.
238	TEM 41	[Nun komm, der Heiden Heiland, K.211] Chorale prelude.
239	HAM 234	[Prelude and fugue, organ, K.141, E major]
240	Scher 249	[Prelude and fugue, organ, K.143, E minor]
241	Hamb 84	[Toccata and fugue, organ, K.157, F major]

242 HAM 190b   ⌐Vater unser im Himmelreich, K.219¬ Chorale prelude.

243 Hamb 77   BYRD, William, 1543-1623.
                    ⌐The bells, virginals¬ Variations.

244 Lern 55   ⌐Carmans whistle, virginals¬ Variations. From My
                    Ladye Nevells book.

245 SS 52   ⌐Fantasia, 5 viols, no.2¬ Browning fantasia.

246 Flor 91   ⌐Galliard, harpsichord¬ From the Fitzwilliam virginal
                    book, v.2.

247 MM 25   ⌐Gradualia, book 2. Ego sum panis vivus¬ Motet.
                    4 voices.

248 HAM 150   ⌐Gradualia, book 2. Non vos relinquam¬ Motet.
                    5 voices.

249 Starr 39   ⌐Look down, O Lord¬ Anthem. 4 voices.

250 HAM 151   ⌐Songs of sundry natures. Christ rising again¬ Verse
                    anthem. 6 voices. No.46 of the collection.

251 Scher 145   ⌐Songs of sundry natures. The nightingale so pleasant¬
                    Madrigal. 3 voices. No.9 of the collection.

                    C'est la fin, 685.

252 Glea 9   C'est la jus.
                    Trouvere rondeau. 13th cent. Voice with chorus.

253 HAM 239   CABANILLES, Juan, 1644-1712.
                    ⌐Paseos, organ¬ Chaconne.

254 RR 140b   CABEZÓN, Antonio de, 1510-1566.
                    ⌐Ave maris stella, organ. 3d verse¬

255 HAM 134   ⌐Diferencias Cavallero¬ Keyboard variations.

256 Scher 113   ⌐Fuga al contrario, organ¬ Ricercar.

257 Flor 76   ⌐Intermedio para Kyrie¬ Organ.

258 Flor 77   ⌐Tiento, organ¬

259 RR 140a   ⌐Versillo del primer tono, no.4, organ¬

260 HAM 133   ⌐Versos, sexto tono¬ 4 organ versets.

261 Flor 99b   CACCINI, Giulio, 1550(ca.)-1618.
                    ⌐L'Euridice. Per quel vago boschetto¬ Voice and con-
                    tinuo. Incomplete.

262 Scher 173   ⌐Le nuove musiche (1602) Amarilli mia bella¬ Voice
     Starr 68   and continuo.

263 Hamb 67   ⌐Le nuove musiche (1602) Arde il mio petto¬ Voice and
     Scher 172   continuo.

264 Lern 62   ⌐Le nuove musiche (1602) Dolcissimo sospiro¬ Voice
                    and continuo.

265 MM 30   ⌐Le nuove musiche (1602) Dovrò dunque morire¬ Voice
                    and lute.

266 Wolf 49   ⌐Le nuove musiche (1602) Io parto¬ Voice and continuo.

267 Flor 97 ⌐Le nuove musiche (1602) Perfidissimo volto⌐ Madrigal.
Voice and continuo.

268 HAM 184 ⌐Le nuove musiche (1602) Sfogava con le stelle⌐
Voice and continuo.

269 Scher 116 CADÉAC, Pierre, 16th cent.
⌐Je suis déshéritée⌐ Chanson. 4 voices.

Cadmus et Hermione, 967.

Caduta de' Decemviri, 1367.

270 Wolf 38 CAIMO, Giuseppe, ca.1540-1584.
⌐Madrigals, book 4. È ben ragion⌐ 5 voices.

271 Scher 273 CALDARA, Antonio, 1630-1736.
⌐Stabat mater. Selections⌐ Opening 4-part chorus
(Stabat mater) and aria for 4 soloists (Quis est homo)
With orchestra.

272 OM 49 Caligo terrae scinditur.
Petronian motet. English, early 14th cent. 3 voices.
Polytext: Caligo terrae; Virgo Maria; textless tenor.

273 Scher 160 CALVISIUS, Seth, 1556-1650.
⌐Ein' feste Burg⌐ Chorale setting. 3 voices.

274 Scher 222 CAMBERT, Robert, d.1677.
⌐Pomone. Ah ma soeur⌐ Recitative, act 1, scene 2.
3 solo voices with continuo.

275 HAM 223 ⌐Pomone. Overture⌐ 4 stringed instruments.

276 Scher 306 CAMERLOHER, Placidus Cajetanus Laurentius von, 1718-1782.
⌐Symphony, string orchestra, C major. Andante⌐

277 Wolf 26 Caminata.
4 instruments. 16th cent.

278 Wolf 51 CAMPION, Thomas, 1567-1620.
⌐Airs (1601) I care not for these ladies⌐ Voice with
lute and bass viol.

279 HAM 257 CAMPRA, André, 1660-1744.
⌐Cantate Domino⌐ Motet. 2 voices with continuo.

Le carnaval de Vénise. see his ⌐Fêtes vénitiennes⌐

280 TEM 45 ⌐Les fêtes vénitiennes. Chaconne⌐ String orchestra.
In later productions of the opera, this chaconne became
the 2d entrée, with the title L'amour saltimbanque.

281 Scher 261 ⌐Les fêtes vénitiennes. Quelle audace⌐ Recitative and
aria, act 3, scene 2. 2 soloists with continuo.

Can vei la lauzeta, 175.

282 HAM 28i Candida virginitas.
Motet. ca.1250. 2 voices. Polytext: Candida; Flos
Filius. Notre Dame school. With related clausula and
French motet.

Canova, Francesco. see FRANCESCO da Milano

Cantate Domino, 279, 909.

Cantigas de Santa Maria, 40-48.

Canto carnascialesco, 1152.

Canzona dopo l'epistola, 560.

283 MM 26 Canzona per l'epistola.
Keyboard instrument. Early 17th cent.

284 Scher 180 CAPELLO, Giovanni Francesco, b.ca.1585.
⌐Abraham⌐ Dialogo. Solo voices with chorus and instruments.

285 TEM 21 CAPIROLA, Vincenzo, b.1474.
⌐O mia cieca e dura sorte, lute⌐ Shown with the
Cara 4-voiced frottola version (see 287).

286 Hamb 54 CARA, Marco, fl.1500.
⌐Defecerunt⌐ Frottola. 4 voices.

287 Min 50 ⌐Non è tempo d'aspettare⌐ Frottola. 4 voices.
(see 205 for a lute arrangement)

288 TEM 20 ⌐O mia cieca e dura sorte⌐ Frottola. 4 voices.
With a lute version by Capirola underlaid (see 284).

289 Lern 38 ⌐Ochi mei lassi⌐ Strambotto (frottola) 4 voices.

290 RR 33a ⌐Oimè il cor⌐ Frottola. 4 voices.

Cara la vita, 1040, 1617.

Cara sposa, 730.

291 Lern 5 Carissime: Apparuit gratia Dei.
Epistle. Gregorian chant.

292 Hamb 93 CARISSIMI, Giacomo, 1605-1674.
⌐Ezechia. Selections⌐ Aria (Dextera Domini) and
5-part chorus (Narrabimus omnes).

293 Scher 198 ⌐Jephte. Selections⌐ Scene from the oratorio.

294 Flor 129 ⌐Jephte. Hymnum cantemus⌐ 2 voices and continuo.

295 Lern 68 ⌐Jephte. Plorate filii⌐ Final chorus with preceding
Starr 85 recitatives. Solo voices, 6-part chorus, and continuo.

296 HAM 207 ⌐Jonas. Miserunt ergo sortem⌐ Recitative, with chorus
and continuo.

297 MM 32 ⌐Judicium Salomonis. Afferte gladium⌐ Scene from the
oratorio. Recitative. 3 solo voices and continuo.

Carmans whistle, 244.

Carmina chromatica, 914.

Carnaval de Vénise, 280-281.

Carpentras. see GENET, Elzéar

Caserta... see ANTONELLO da Caserta

Castor et Pollux, 1296-1299.

298 Glea 3   Catholic Church. Liturgy and ritual.
                ⌐Mass, Easter Sunday¬ The proper and ordinary of the
                mass. Gregorian chant.

299 OM 11   Catholic Church. Liturgy and ritual. Salisbury.
                ⌐Mass, Easter Sunday¬ With diagram of the Salisbury
                Cathedral. Gregorian chant.

300 OM 10   Catholic Church. Liturgy and ritual. Salisbury.
                Procession before Mass of the Day on Easter. Gregorian
                chant.

301 Flor 95   CAVALIERI, Emilio de', 1550(ca.)-1602.
                ⌐Godi, turba mortal¬ Madrigal. Voice and guitar.

302 Scher 170   ⌐Io piango Filli¬ Aria cantata e sonata, al modo anti-
                co. Tenor and 2 flutes.

303 Scher 169   ⌐Rappresentazione di anima e di corpo. Selections¬
                Solo voices and chorus, with continuo.

304 HAM 183   ⌐Rappresentazione di anima e di corpo. A questi suoni¬
                Recitative and 3-part chorus, with continuo.

305 TEM 37   ⌐Rappresentazione di anima e di corpo. Act 2. Selec-
                tions¬ Scene from the middle of act 2 of the opera.
                Soloists and chorus with continuo.

306 Flor 94   ⌐Rappresentazione di anima e di corpo. Il tempo fuge¬
                Recitative from act 1, scene 1. Voice with continuo.

                Cavallero, 255.

307 Flor 126   CAVALLI, Pier Francesco, 1602-1676.
                ⌐L'Erismena. Vaghe stelle¬ Aria from act 2, scene 1.
                With continuo.

308 Scher 201   ⌐Il Giasone. Dell'antro magico¬ Act 1, scene 15.
                Medea's aria and recitative.

309 SS 32   ⌐L'Ormindo. Selections¬ Duet (Se nel sen di giovinet-
                ti) from act 1 and death scene (Io moro) from act 2.
                With continuo.

310 Scher 200   ⌐L'Ormindo. Io moro¬ Death scene. Recitative.
                2 voices with continuo.

311 HAM 206   ⌐Il Serse. Ecco la lettra¬ Recitative and aria.

312 Scher 103   CAVAZZONI, Girolamo, 1520(ca.)-1560.
                ⌐Ad coenam agni providi, organ¬ Easter hymn. From his
                Intavolatura (1542)

313 Flor 71   ⌐Ave maris stella, organ¬ Intonazione. Includes the
                Gregorian chant.

314 HAM 118   ⌐Falte d'argens, organ¬ Canzona. From his Intavola-
                tura.

315 HAM 117   ⌐Missa apostolorum, organ¬ From his Intavolatura.

316 RR 123   ⌐Missa de Beata Virgine, organ. Mariam gubernans¬
                A setting of the trope. Includes the plainsong.

317 HAM 116   ⌐Ricercar, organ, F major¬ From his Intavolatura.

318 Flor 70 ⌈Ricercar, organ, G major⌉

319 HAM 219 CAZZATI, Maurizio, 1620(ca.)-1677.
⌈Sonata, violin & continuo, op.55, no.1, D minor⌉ La
Pellicana.

Ce fut en mai, 1038.

Ce j'eusse fait, 901.

Cecchina nubile, 1238.

320 HAM 227 CEREROLS, Joan, 1618-1676.
⌈Señor mio Jesu Cristo⌉ Villancico. 4 voices and
continuo.

321 Ein 16 CERTON, Pierre, 1510(ca.)-1572.
⌈Je ne l'ose dire⌉ Chanson. 4 voices.

322 Wolf 8 CESARIS, Johannes, fl.1400-1417.
⌈Bonté bialté⌉ 3 voices. Without text.

323 Scher 203 CESTI, Antonio, 1623-1669.
⌈L'Argia. Alma mia⌉ Da capo aria, with instrumental
ensemble.

324 Hamb 70 ⌈Il pomo d'oro. Ah quanto è vero⌉ Aria from act 2,
scene 9. With strings and continuo.

325 HAM 221 ⌈Il pomo d'oro. Di bellezza e di valore⌉ Chorus and
ritornello from act 4, scene 12.

326 Starr 81 ⌈Il pomo d'oro. E dove t'aggiri⌉ Aria, from act 1,
scene 1.

327 Flor 132 ⌈Il pomo d'oro. Nò, il pomo nò⌉ Terzetto, act 1,
scene 5. With continuo.

328 Scher 202 ⌈Il pomo d'oro. Sonata⌉ Overture. Instrumental ensemble.

Cesti, Marc Antonio. see CESTI, Antonio

Cesti, Pietro. see CESTI, Antonio

Cetra, 1580.

329 Flor 127 CHAMBONNIÈRES, Jacques Champion de, 1602(ca.)-1672.
Hamb 78 ⌈Pièces de clavessin. Allemande, La rare⌉

330 HAM 212 ⌈Pièces de clavessin. Chaconne, F major⌉

331 Flor 127 ⌈Pièces de clavessin. Gigue en canon⌉

332 Scher 218 ⌈Pièces de clavessin. Sarabande, Jeunes zéphirs⌉ With
Double.

333 Ein 9 Chanconnete, va t'en tost.
Motet. 13th cent. 3 voices. Polytext: Chanconnete;
A la cheminee; Veritatem.

Chant des oyseaux, 823.

Chanterai por mon coraige, 714.

Charmante nuit, 209.

334 Lern 70   CHARPENTIER, Marc Antoine, d.1704.
                 [Ave regina coelorum, H.22] Motet. 2 sopranos and
                 continuo.

335 HAM 226   [Dialogus inter Magdalenam et Jesum, H.423. Hei mihi
                 infelix Magdalena] Recitative.
                   (HAM mistakenly indicates that the Dialogus is part
                   of the composer's Reniement de saint-Pierre.)

336 TEM 42   [Le reniement de saint-Pierre, H.424. Selections]
                 Peter's denial scene from the oratorio. Soloists and
                 5-part chorus.

                 Che più si tarda omai, 738.

                 Cheshire, 527.

337 Lern 13   Chevalier mult estes guariz.
                   Trouvère rotrouenge.

                 Chi la gagliarda, 448.

                 Chi più le vuol sapere, 889.

                 Chionoblepharou pater, 1021.

                 Chominciamento di gioia, 515.

                 Choralis Constantinus, 804.

                 Chosi pensoso, 890.

338 Scher 75   Christ ist erstanden.
                   Tower chorale. 4 brass instruments. From Peter
                   Schoeffer's Liederbuch, 1513.

                 Christ ist erstanden, 338, 1466.

                 Christ lag in Todesbanden, 106-107, 125, 1155, 1594-1595.

                 Christ rising again, 250.

                 Christ unser Herr zum Jordan kam, 234.

339 Lern 8   Christe redemptor omnium.
                   Hymn. Gregorian chant. 11th cent.?

                 Christi gebet auf dem Ölberg, 181.

                 Christi Geburt, 180.

                 Christi redemptor omnium, 468.

                 Christmas concerto, 364.

340 HAM 17b   Christo psallat.
                   Conductus in rondeau form, 12th cent.

                 Christus filius Dei, 805.

                 Christus hat uns ein Vorbild gelassen, 672.

                 Christus hunc diem, 1106.

                 Chrysea phorminx, 1242.

341 HAM 55   CICONIA, Johannes, fl.1400-1411.
                 [Et in terra pax] 3 voices. Isolated mass movement.
                   (Not the same work as Scher 29)

342 Scher 29 ⌜Et in terra pax⌝ 3 voices. Isolated mass movement. (Not the same work as HAM 55)

343 OM 73 ⌜Sus une fontayne⌝ Virelai. 3 voices.

Ciel protège les héros, 961.

344 OM 46 Cil s'entremet. Motet. French, ca.1250. 3 voices. Polytext: Cil s'entremet; Nus hom; Victimae paschali.

345 Scher 101 CIMELLO, Tomaso, 16th cent. ⌜Gli occhi tuoi⌝ Villanesca. 3 voices.

Cimento dell'armonia e dell'invenzione, 1581-1583.

Ciz chans, 529.

Clemens non Papa. see CLÉMENT, Jacques

Clemens rector, 878.

346 HAMB 40b CLÉMENT, Jacques, 16th cent. ⌜Missa, Panis quem ego dabo. Kyrie I⌝ 4 voices.

347 Hamb 37 ⌜Souterliedekens. Als ick riep met verlanghen⌝ Psalm 4. 3 voices.

348 Flor 69 ⌜Souterliedekens. Vrolick en bly loeft god⌝
RR 79 Psalm 65 (66) 3 voices.

349 HAM 125 ⌜Vox in Rama audita est⌝ Motet. 4 voices.

350 HAM 200 COELHO, Manuel Rodrigues, b.1583. ⌜Flores de música. Verso do primeiro tom⌝ Voice and organ.

Coetus venit heroicus, 64.

Combat des éléments, 210.

Combattimento à David e Goliath, 871.

Combattimento di Tancredi e Clorinda, 1044.

Come away sweet love, 673.

Come my dearest, 87.

Comfort ye my people, 724.

Comme femme, 23, 433, 1430.

Comment au'a moy, 690.

351 Flor 49 COMPÈRE, Loyset, 1455(ca.)-1518.
RR 42 ⌜Crucifige⌝ Motet. 4 voices.

352 Amb 25 ⌜Nous sommes de l'ordre de St. Babouin⌝ Chanson. 4 voices.

353 HAM 79 ⌜Royne du ciel⌝ Rondeau. 3 voices.

Componimenti musicali, 1078-1079.

Compostela school. see Part 2: Subjects

Comus, 924.

Con brachi assai, 643.

Con dolce brama, 1240.

354 Flor 75 Conde claros.
Variations. 16th cent. Lute.

Conditor alme siderum, 469.

355 Flor 23 Congaudeant catholici.
Organum. 12th cent. Compostela school.

Congaudeant catholici, 37, 355.

Congoxa más, 500.

Conlonba candid'e gentile, 891.

Conosco, 1203.

Consolation aux amis du Sr. Lenclos, 618.

Consonanze stravaganti, 976.

356 Wolf 1 Constantes estote.
Antiphon. Organum (responsory) 14th cent. 2 voices.
Incomplete.

357 Scher 274 CONTI, Francesco Bartolomeo, 1681-1732.
[Griselda. Introduzione. Minuet] Instrumental ensemble.

358 Scher 91 Contre raison.
Canzona, keyboard. (Attaingnant, 1530).

Conversione di Sant'Agostino, 747-748.

Conviviorum deliciae, 408.

359 HAM 86b COOPER.
[I have been a foster] English song, ca.1500.
3 voices.

Cor mio, deh non laguire, 972.

360 HAM 48a CORDIER, Baude, 15th cent.
[Amans ames] Rondeau. 3 voices.

361 HAM 48b [Belle bonne, sage] Rondeau. 3 voices.

362 OM 98 [Se cuer d'amant] Rondeau. 3 voices.

363 Starr 105 CORELLI, Arcangelo, 1653-1713.
[Concerto grosso, op.6, no.3, C minor] Strings and
continuo.

364 SS 53 [Concerto grosso, op.6, no.8, G minor] Christmas concerto. Strings and continuo.

365 HAM 252 [Sonata, violin & continuo, op.5, no.3, C major. Se-
lections] 1st and 2d movements.

366 HAM 253 [Sonata, violin & continuo, op.5, no.8, E minor]

367 Scher 240 [Trio-sonata, violins & continuo, op.2, no.2, D minor]

368 Lern 76 [Trio-sonata, violins & continuo, op.3, no.2, D major]

369	MM 39 Nort 6	⌈Trio-sonata, violins & continuo, op.3, no.7, E minor⌉
370	Hamb 89	⌈Trio-sonata, violins & continuo, op.3, no.9, F minor⌉
371	Nort3 18	⌈Trio-sonata, violins & continuo, op.4, no.1, C major⌉
372	Flor 143	⌈Trio-sonata, violins & continuo, op.4, no.6, E major⌉

Corispero, 1468.

Cornysh, Robert. see CORNYSHE, William

373 HAM 86a   CORNYSHE, William, 1468(ca.)-1523.
⌈A dew, my hartis lust⌉ English song. 3 voices.
(HAM probably errs in using forename Robert)

374 RR 176   ⌈Hey, Robyn, joly Robyn⌉ 3 voices, 2 of them in canon.

Coro di ninfe e pastori, 1050.

375 Scher 99   CORTECCIA, Francesco Bernardo, 1504-1571.
⌈O begl'anni dell'oro⌉ Madrigal. Tenor with gamba.
From the Florentine wedding music of 1539.

Costanza e fortezza, 583.

376 HAM 147   COSTELEY, Guillaume, 1531-1606.
⌈Musique. Allon, gay Bergeres⌉ Chanson. 4 voices.

377 Flor 153   COUPERIN, François, 1668-1733.
⌈Leçons des ténèbres. No.2. Recordata est Jerusalem⌉
Aria with continuo. Includes the melisma.

378 Scher 264   ⌈Pièces de clavecin, 1. livre. Selections⌉ La fleurie
(1. ordre), and Allemande La ténébreuse (3. ordre).

379 Starr 116   ⌈Pièces de clavecin, 1. livre, 1. ordre. L'auguste⌉
Allemande.

380 Flor 152   ⌈Pièces de clavecin, 2. livre, 12. ordre. La galante⌉
    MM 40

381 HAM 265a   ⌈Pièces de clavecin, 3. livre, 14. ordre. Le rossignol
en amour⌉

382 HAM 265b   ⌈Pièces de clavecin, 3. livre, 18. ordre. Soeur
Monique⌉

383 Flor 152   ⌈Pièces de clavecin, 4. livre, 21. ordre. La reine des
coeurs⌉

384 HAM 266   ⌈Qui dat nivem⌉ Motet. Solo voice with instrumental
ensemble.

385 HAM 229   COUPERIN, Louis, 1626(ca.)-1661.
⌈Menuet de Poitou, harpsichord⌉

386 OM 92   COUSIN, mid-15th cent.
⌈Missa tubae. Sanctus⌉ 4 voices.

Cousser, Johann Sigismund. see KUSSER, JS

Creatura gentile, 815.

387   MM 20   CRECQUILLON, Thomas, d.1557.
                   ⌈Pour ung plaisir⌉ Polyphonic chanson. 4 voices.
                   Keyboard version by Andrea Gabrieli underlaid.

388   Scher 118   ⌈Quand me souvient⌉ Chanson. Voice with lute.

                     Credo, 389, 937, 1257.

389   SS 4a   Credo I.
                   Gregorian chant, 9th cent.

                     Crispinus. see STAPPEN, Crispin van

                     Crist and Sainte Marie, 656.

                     Croesus, 841-844.

390   HAM 268   CROFT, William, 1678-1727.
                   ⌈Put me not to rebuke⌉ Anthem. 6 voices. Abridged.

                     Crucifige, 351.

                     Cruda Amarilli, 1047.

                     Cruda morte, 1207.

391   Scher 208   CRÜGER, Johann, 1598-1662.
                   ⌈Schmücke dich, o liebe Seele⌉ Abendsmahlslied.
                   Voice and continuo.

392   OM 2   Crux fidelis and Pange lingua.
                   Refrain and hymn for feasts of the Holy Cross. Galli-
                   can chant, 6th cent.

                     Cueur angoisseux, 155.

                     Cuidoient li losengier, 713.

393   Flor 5   Cum invocarem exaudivit.
                   Psalm 4. Gregorian chant.

                     Cum jubilo, 879.

                     Cunctipotens. see also Kyrie

394   SS 2a   Cunctipotens.
                   Gregorian chant, 10th cent. Kyrie from Mass Ordinary
                   IV.

395   SS 2b   Cunctipotens.
                   Organ setting of the Kyrie. 14th cent. Incomplete.

                     Cunctipotens, 394-399, 1032-1033, 1535.

396   RMA 41   Cunctipotens dominator.
                   Kyrie trope, Gregorian.

397   Hamb 4   Cunctipotens genitor.
                   Kyrie trope, Gregorian.

398   Flor 22   Cunctipotens genitor.
      HAM 27b   Melismatic organum. ca.1125. 2 voices. Compostela
      Hamb 14   school.

399   Flor 21   Cunctipotens genitor.
      Glea 30   Organum. Kyrie. 11th cent. 2 voices.
      HAM 26a
      Hamb 13
      Scher 9

D'une coline, 942.

Da chi spero, 1470.

Da Jakob nu das Kleid ansah, 1431.

Da Jesus an dem Kreuze stund, 1388, 1420.

Da le belle contrade, 1331.

Da me non speri, 607.

Dafne, 602-603.

Dal male il bene, 7.

400   HAM 99a   DALZA, Joanambrosio.
                   [Tastar de corde con il ricercar dietro, lute] ca.1500.

Dame, merci, 1504.

Dame mon cuer, 691.

Dame, par vous, 706.

401   HAM 64   DAMETT, early 15th cent.
                   [Beata Dei genitrix] Hymn. 2 solo voices and 3-part
                   chorus.

Dance of death, 8.

Danceries, 624-626.

402   Lern 10-11   Daniel (Liturgical drama) Selections.
                   Vos qui paretix and Hic verus Dei, from The play of
                   Daniel. 12th cent. Solo voices.

403   HAM 162   DANIEL, John, ca.1565-1630.
                   [Songs for the lute, viol and voice. Stay, cruel,
                   stay]

Dans un jour de triomphe, 964.

Danse royale, 516.

Danserye, 1472.

Dappoi che'l sole, 1099.

Dardanus, 1300-1301.

Dascanio, Josquin. see DEPRÈS, Josquin

Daz Gedeones wollenvlius, 1342.

De antequera sale el moro, 580.

De bon espoir, 692.

404   MM 11   De castitatis thalamo.
                   Conductus.

De' dinmi tu che, 892.

De lamentatione Hieremiae, 1171.

405 OM 41   De monte lapis.
Organum (partly discant style) 2 voices. St. Martial school.

406 Flor 62   De no, de si, de no.
Frottola. Late 15th cent. 4 voices. From Petrucci's Frottole, libro 5 (1505)

De plus en plus, 186.

De profundis, 589, 915.

407 Ein 3   De quinque panibus.
Antiphon. Gregorian chant.

De se debent, 1037.

De souspirant cuer, 709.

De toutes flours, 693.

Deba contre mes debateurs, 666, 941.

Decantabat populus Israel, 1564.

Defecerunt, 286.

Deh ferm' amor, 533.

Deh lascia, o core, 201.

Deich von der guoten schiet, 178.

Del sieu tort farai esmenda, 1193.

Delitiae testudinis, 1319-1320.

Dell'antro magico, 308.

Delphin de música, 1087.

408 Scher 154   DEMANTIUS, Christoph, 1567-1643.
⌈Conviviorum deliciae. Es ist nit zu ermessen⌉ Intrada. 6 voices.

409 HAM 32c   Deo confitemini.
Motet. 13th cent. 3 voices. Polytext: Deo...; Deo confitemini; Domino ⌈Hec dies⌉

410 Scher 32b   Deo gracias Anglia.
Carol. English, ca.1415.

Déploration sur la mort de J. Okeghem, 416.

411 Scher 61   DEPRÈS, Josquin, d.1521.
⌈A l'heure que je voux p.x.⌉ Canonic chanson. 4 instruments.

412 Amb 17   ⌈Adieu mes amours⌉ Chanson. 4 voices.

413 Hamb 34   ⌈Ave Maria gratia plena⌉ Motet. 4 voices.
Lern 37
MM 19
Nort 1

414 SS 49   ⌈Baisiez moy⌉ Chanson. Double canon. 4 voices.

415	Scher 62b	[La Bernardina] Canzona. 3 instruments.
416	Nort3 6	[Déploration sur la mort de Johan Okeghem] 5 voices.
417	Wolf 19	[Fantasia, 3 instruments]
418	HAM 91	[Faulte d'argent] Polyphonic chanson. 5 voices.
419	Scher 71	[El grillo] Frottola. 4 voices.
420	HAM 95b	[In te Domine] Frottola. 4 voices.
421	Amb 15	[Jai bien cause] Chanson. 6 voices.
422	Amb 16	[Je sey bien dire] Chanson. 4 voices.
423	Nort3 8	[Missa, L'homme armé. Agnus Dei] 4 voices. Includes the original tune.
424	HAM 89 Hamb 35	[Missa, L'homme armé. Agnus Dei II] "Ex una voce tres". Mensuration canon. 3 voices.
425	Scher 59	[Missa la sol fa re mi. Selections] Et incarnatus and Crucifixus. 4 voices.
426	Amb 14	[Missa, Pange lingua] 4 voices. Includes the chant.
427	Flor 50b	[Missa, Pange lingua. Agnus Dei I] 4 voices.
428	SS 4d	[Missa, Pange lingua. Credo] 4 voices.
429	Starr 30	[Missa, Pange lingua. Gloria] 4 voices.
430	Scher 60	[O domine Jesu Christe] Passionsmotette. 4 male voices.
431	Flor 51	[Petite Camusette] Polyphonic chanson. 6 voices.
432	Amb 18 Nort3 7	[Scaramella] 4 voices.
433	Amb 13	[Stabat mater] Motet. 5 voices. Tenor melody is Comme femme.
434	HAM 90	[Tu pauperum refugium] Motet. 4 voices.
435	Scher 62a	[Vive le roy] Canon. 4 brass instruments.
		Descende in hortum, 535.
436	Starr 16	Descendit de coelis. Organum. 3 voices. Notre Dame school.
		Desolata mater, 530.
		Des Près, Josquin. see DEPRÈS, Josquin
		Detractor est, 531.
		Deus autem noster, 788.
437	OM 52	Deus in adjutorium. Conductus. French, early 13th cent. 3 voices.
438	OM 3a	Deus miserere. Preces from Office for the dead. Mozarabic chant. (Differs somewhat from RMA 21)

439 RMA 21   Deus miserere.
                   Preces from the Office of the Dead. Mozarabic chant,
                   7th cent.

                 Deus noster refugium, 1591.

440 Lern 4   Deus qui hanc sacratissimam.
                   Collect. Gregorian chant.

                 Deutsche Sprüche von Leben und Tod, 931.

                 Devin du village, 1341.

                 Dex est ausi comme li pellicans, 1505.

                 Dextera Domini, 292.

                 Di bellezza e di valore, 325.

                 Di novo è giunt' un cavalier, 817.

                 Dialoghi e sonetti, 1009.

                 Dialogi zwischen Gott..., 741.

                 Dialogus inter Magdalenam et Jesum, 335.

441 RMA 20   Dicet Domino.
                   Confractorium. Ambrosian chant.

                 Dido and Aeneas, 1274-1277.

                 Die mit Tränen säen, 1609.

442 Starr 10   Dies irae.
                   Sequence. Gregorian chant.

443 Scher 89b   Dieu aiude a paures gens.
                   Provençal song, ca.1525. 1 voice.

                 Diex soit, 9.

                 Dimmi un poco che vuol dire, 1223.

                 Diocletiano, 1184.

                 Dirai vos senes doptansa, 983.

444 Scher 150   DŁUGORAJ, Wojciech, 1557 or 8-ca.1619.
                   ⌈Fantasia, lute⌉

                 Dodecacorde, 941.

                 Dolce mia fiamma, 1426.

                 Dolcissima mia vita, 627.

                 Dolcissimo sospiro, 264.

445 HAM 28g   Dominator Domine.
     Hamb 19   Motet. ca. 1225. 3 voices. Polytext: Dominator Do-
                   mine; Ecce ministerium; Domino. Notre Dame school.

                 Domine ad adjuvandum, 1058.

                 Domine Deus rex celestis, 1057.

                 Domine, ne in furore tuo, 916.

                 Domino, 94, 409, 445, 1271.

446 HAM 28f   Domino fidelium.
            Motet. ca.1225. 2 voices. Notre Dame school.

447 Lern 1   Dominus dixit.
            Introit. Gregorian chant.

448 Flor 87   DONATO, Baldassare, d.1603.
            ⌐Chi la gagliarda⌐ Villanesca. 4 voices.

449 Wolf 46   ⌐Viva sempre in ogni etate⌐ Villanesca. 4 voices.
            From the Primo libro di canzon villanesche, 1551.

450 Wolf 45   Donne, venite al ballo.
            Balletto. 16th cent. 4 voices.

451 Lern 57   DOWLAND, John, 1563-1626.
            ⌐Flow my teares, lute⌐

452 Flor 106   ⌐Songs or airs, book 1. My thoughts are winged with
            hope⌐ Madrigal. 4 voices.

453 Ein 23   ⌐Songs or airs, book 1. My thoughts are winged with
   TEM 34   hope⌐ Voice with lute.

454 Scher 146   ⌐Songs or airs, book 1. Now I needs must part⌐ Ayre.
            4 voices.

455 Lern 56   ⌐Songs or airs, book 2. Flow, my tears⌐ Voice with
   SS 22   lute.

456 HAM 163   ⌐Songs or airs, book 3. What if I never speed⌐ Ver-
            sions for soprano and lute and for 4 voices.

457 Scher 226   DRAGHI, Antonio, 1635-1700.
            ⌐La pazienza di Socrate. Act 1, scene 2⌐ Recitatives
            and duets. With continuo.

458 Amb 34   DUCIS, Benedictus, fl.1532.
            ⌐Motets. Selections⌐ Sechs geistliche deutsche Lieder.
            4 voices. German texts.

459 Glea 57   Ductia.
   HAM 40a   French, 13th cent. 1 instrument.

460 HAM 41b   Ductia.
            13th cent. 2 instruments.

461	HAM 68	DUFAY, Guillaume, d.1474. ⌐Adieu m'amour⌐ Rondeau. 3 voices.
462	Nort3 4	⌐Alma redemptoris mater, 3 voices⌐ Motet.
463	HAM 65	⌐Alma redemptoris mater, 4 voices⌐ Antiphon B.M.V. (motet).
464	Scher 38	⌐Aures ad nostras deitatis⌐ Hymn. 3 voices.
465	Lern 33	⌐Ave maris stella⌐ Hymn. Fauxbourdon. 3 voices.
466	OM 99	⌐Belle, veullies moy retenir⌐ Rondeau. 3 voices.
467	Hamb 32	⌐Bon jour, bon mois⌐ Chanson. 3 voices.
468	RR 22	⌐Christi redemptor omnium⌐ Christmas hymn. Odd stan- zas unison chant; even for 3 voices, with and without fauxbourdon.
469	Min 24	⌐Conditor alme siderum⌐ Hymn. 3 voices.
470	Starr 27	⌐Iste confessor⌐ Hymn. Fauxbourdon. 3 voices.
471	Scher 40	⌐Le jour s'endort⌐ Chanson. Voice and 2 instruments.
472	OM 89	⌐Kyrie⌐ From a Kyrie-Gloria-Credo setting. 3 voices.
473	Flor 44	⌐Malheureux cueur⌐ Virelai. Voice and 2 instruments.
474	Flor 43	⌐Missa, Ave Maria coelorum. Sanctus⌐ 4 voices.
475	Lern 34	⌐Missa caput. Agnus Dei⌐ 4 voices.
476	HAM 66b-c Hamb 31	⌐Missa, L'homme armé. Selections⌐ Kyrie I and Agnus III. 4 voices.
477	RR 19	⌐Missa, L'homme armé. Agnus Dei I⌐ 4 voices.
478	Scher 39	⌐Missa, Sancti Jacobi. Kyrie⌐ 2-3 voices.
479	MM 15	⌐Missa, Se la face ay pale. Kyrie I⌐ 4 voices. Includes the tenor of his chanson on the tune.
480	HAM 67	⌐Mon chier amy⌐ Ballade. 3 voices.
481	SS 4c	⌐Pange lingua⌐ Hymn. 3 voices.
482	Wolf 12	⌐Veni creator spiritus⌐ Hymn. 3 voices.
		Dulce lignum, 56-57.
		Dunque ruvida scorza, 602.
483	RMA 126	DUNSTABLE, John, 1370(ca.)-1453. ⌐Alma redemptoris mater⌐ Motet in ballade style. 2-3 voices.
484	Starr 28 Wolf 11	⌐Ave maris stella⌐ Motet. 3 voices.
485	Flor 41	⌐Kyrie⌐ 3 voices.
486	HAM 61	⌐O rosa bella⌐ Song. Voice with 2 instruments.
487	Scher 35	⌐Puisque m'amour⌐ Chanson. 3 voices or instruments.
488	Lern 31 Scher 34	⌐Quam pulcra es⌐ Motet. 3 voices.

489	HAM 62 Hamb 28	⌐Sancta Maria non est⌐ Motet. 3 voices.
490	SS 5b	⌐Sanctus⌐ 2-3 voices. Isolated mass movement; appears as no.13 in the collected works.
491	OM 97	⌐Speciosa facta es⌐ Votive antiphon. Motet. 3 voices.
492	TEM 18	⌐Veni sancte spiritus⌐ Isorhythmic motet. 3 voices.

Durandarte, 1026-1027.

493	HAM 273	DURANTE, Francesco, 1684-1755. ⌐Duetti da camera. Fiero acerbo destin⌐ Voices with keyboard.

Durch Adams Fall, 126.

Durchkläre dich, 1501.

È ben ragion, 270.

E che farete amanti, 7.

494	OM 75	E con chaval. Madrigal. Italian, early 14th cent. 2 voices.

E, dame jolie, 686.

E dove t'aggiri, 326.

E ma dame, 1220.

E quando andarete, 1633.

495	Scher 159	ECCARD, Johann, 1553-1611. ⌐Wach auf, du werte Christenheit⌐ Adventslied. 6 voices. Nr.1 of Preussische Festlieder, 1.Teil.

Ecce ministerium, 445.

Ecce quomodo moritur, 745.

496	Scher 248b	ECCLES, John, d.1735. ⌐Hark Harry, 'tis late⌐ Catch. 3 voices.

Ecco il povero Tracollo, 1200.

Ecco la lettra, 311.

Echo fantasia, 1475.

497	OM 57	Edi beo thu. English song, late 13th cent. 2 voices.

Ego sum panis vivus, 247.

Ego vir, 1334.

Eins bitte ich vom Herrn, 235.

Eius in oriente, 499.

Eja mater, fons amoris, 1205.

Elend du hast umbfangen mich, 954, 1189.

Emendemus in melius, 1059.

En attendant, 1429.

En chantant vueil ma dolor descouvrir, 1506.

498   Glea 12   En mai la rousee.
                     Trouvère lai segment.

499   Flor 28   En non Diu!
      Glea 60   Motet. French, 13th cent. 3 voices. Polytext: En non
      MM 10   Diu; Quant voi la rose; Eius in oriente. Notre Dame
      Starr 18   school.

En regardant, 1536.

Enavois, 1188.

500   HAM 98a   ENCINA, Juan del, 1468-1529?
                     [Congoxa más] Villancico. 4 voices.

501   Flor 57   [Más quiero morir] Villancico. 4 voices.

502   HAM 98c   [Más vale trocar] Villancico. 4 voices.

503   Lern 40   [Oy comamos y bebamos] Villancico. 4 voices.

504   HAM 98b   [Pues que jamás] Villancico. 4 voices.

505   TEM 19   [Soy contento y vos servido] Villancico. 4 voices.

506   RR 130   [Un' amiga tengo] Villancico. 3 voices.

Enfin il est en ma puissance, 965.

Engkainizesthe adelphoi, 832.

507   Glea 11   Enmi! brunette jolie.
                     Trouvère ballade. 13th cent. Voice and chorus.

508   HAM 1a   Entrance hymn for the Emperor.
                     Chinese, ca.1000 BC. 2 instrumental lines.

Erat autem aspectus, 162.

Erindo, 875.

Erismena, 307.

509   Scher 262   ERLEBACH, Philipp Heinrich, 1657-1714.
                     [Harmonische Freude musikalischer Freunde. Fortuna, du
                     scherzest] Da capo aria. Soprano and instrumental en-
                     semble.

510   HAM 254   [Harmonische Freude musikalischer Freude, 2.Teil.
                     Himmel, du weisst meine Plagen] Aria with ritornello.
                     Voice and instrumental ensemble.

Erlösung des menschlichen Geschlechts, 952.

Erntekranz, 768.

Erschienen ist der herrliche Tag, 1397.

511   HAM 10   Eructavit.
                     Verse of the gradual Speciosus forma. Ambrosian and
                     Gregorian chant versions.

Es get gen disem summer, 217.

512   Scher 88b   Es gingen drei Baurn.
                     Song. ca.1540. 4 voices.

Es ist fürwahr ein kostlich Ding, 1416.

Es ist genug, 124.

Es ist nit zu ermessen, 408.

Es leit ein Schloss, 647.

Es taget vor dem Walde, 1438.

Es war ein wunderlicher Krieg, 106.

Es war einmal ein junge Weib, 1458.

| 513 | Amb 61 | ESCOBEDO, Vartolomé, d.1563.
[Introitus in Dominica in sexagesima] Motet. 4 voices. |
| 514 | HAM 8a | Esose laon thaumaturgon despotes.
Ode for Christmas. Byzantine chant, 13th cent. |

Espris d'ire, 711.

Estampie. see also Saltarello; RAIMBAUT

515	OM 86	Estampie. Chominciamento di gioia. Italian, 14th cent. 1 instrument.
516	HAM 40b	Estampie. Danse royale. 13th cent. 1 instrument.
517	Flor 30 HAM 40c Min 18	Estampie. English, 13th cent. 1 instrument.
518	OM 84	Estampie. English, ca.1325. Keyboard.
519	HAM 58	Estampie. English, ca.1325. Organ.
520	HAM 59a Hamb 41 Scher 28	Estampie. Lamento di Tristano. Italian, 14th cent. 1 instrument.
521	Scher 28	Estampie. La manfredina. Italian, 14th cent. 1 instrument.
522	OM 36	Estampie. La quinte estampie real. French, 13th cent. 1 instrument.
523	Glea 55 HAM 41a	Estampie. Stantipes. English, 13th cent. 2 instruments.
524	Glea 56 MM 12 Starr 14	Estampie. Stantipes (ductia) English, 13th cent. 2 instruments.

Estro armonico, 1584-1586.

Et gaudebit, 781, 786, 1287.

Et gaudebit cor vestrum, 705.

Et in terra pax, 341-342.

Et non est qui adjuvet, 704.

Euridice, 261, 1207-1212.

Every valley, 725.

Ewiger Gott, 1432.

Exaudi me, Domine, 1565.

525 OM 48   Excelsus in numine.
    Motet using voice exchange. English, late 13th cent.
    3 voices. Polytext: Excelsus in numine; Benedictus
    Dominus; textless tenor.

Eximie pater, 1270.

Exsultate Deo, 1172.

Exurge Domine, 847.

Ey ich sach in dem Trone, 557.

Ez ist hiute eyn wunnychlicher tac, 1485.

Ezechia, 292.

Fa metter bando, 893.

Factus est, 30.

Fahret wohl, 846.

Fairy queen, 1278.

Falai miña amor, 1028.

Fall of Phaeton, 87.

Falla con misuras, 683.

Fallace speranza, 1427.

Falte d'argens, 314.

526 Flor 73   Fantasia sobre fa-mi-ut-re.
    Spanish, 16th cent. Lute.

527 RR 187   FARMER, John, fl. 1591-1601.
    [Psalm 146] 4 voices. Set to the tune Cheshire.

528 MM 29   FARNABY, Giles, 1565(ca.)-1640.
    [Loth to depart, virginals] Variations.

Faulte d'argent, 418.

529 Glea 79   Fauvel. Bon vin doit.
    Motet. 3 voices. Polytext: Bon vin doit; Quant je le
    voi; Ciz chans.

530 Glea 77   Fauvel. Desolata mater.
    Motet. 3 voices. Polytext: Desolata mater; Quae nutri-
    tos; Filios enutrivi.

531 HAM 43   Fauvel. Detractor est.
    Isorhythmic motet. 3 voices. Polytext: Detractor est;
    Qui secuntur; Verbum iniquum.

Faux Lord, 1239.

Felber sprach, 1402.

Fenice fu, 818.

532 Wolf 61   FERRABOSCO, Alfonso, 1575(ca.)-1628.
     [Aria a 4] Canzonetta. 4 instruments. Published in Simpson's Taffelconsort, 1621.

533 Hamb 48a   FERRABOSCO, Domenico Maria, 1513-1574.
     [Deh ferm' amor] Madrigal. 4 voices.

534 HAM 129   FESTA, Costanzo, d.1545.
     [Quando ritrova] Madrigal. 4 voices.

Feste Burg ist unser Gott, 109-110, 273, 980, 1024, 1591.

Fêtes vénitiennes, 280-281.

535 Amb 31   FEVIN, Antoine de, 1474-1512.
     [Descende in hortum] Motet. 4 voices.

536 HAM 106   [Missa, Mente tota. Agnus Dei] 4 voices.

Fiero acerbo destin, 493.

Figlio, ascolta, 1500.

Figlio, dove t'ascondo, 1369.

Files à marier, 188.

Fili mi, Absalon, 1422.

Filiae Jerusalem, 1116.

Filios enutrivi, 530.

Filosofo di campagna, 607-608.

537 Scher 57   FINCK, Heinrich, 1445-1527.
     [Chorale prelude, G major] ca.1490.

538 Flor 52   [Mag das gesein] 4 voices.

539 Amb 35   [Missa de Beata Virgine] 3 voices.

540 Scher 87   [O schönes Weib] Song. Voice with 3 instruments.

541 HAM 80   [Veni sancte spiritus] Quodlibet. 4 voices. Poly-text: Veni sancte...; Veni creator spiritus.

Fines amouretes, 10.

Fiori musicali, 560-562.

542 Scher 255   FISCHER, Johann, 1646-ca.1721.
     [Tafel-Musik. Suite, 4 instruments, C minor. Marches 1-2]

543 HAM 247   FISCHER, Johann Kaspar Ferdinand, 1665(ca.)-1746.
   Scher 265   [Ariadne musica. Prelude and fugue, organ, E major]

544 Flor 140   [Ariadne musica. Prelude and fugue, organ, E-flat major]

545 Ein 34   [Musicalische Blumen-Büschlein. Suite, harpsichord,
   HAM 248   A minor]

Fitzwilliam virginal book, 227-228, 246, 1065, 1081.

Fleurie, 378.

Flora, 866.

Florentinus, Alexander. see ALESSANDRO da Firenze

Flores de música, 350.

Florilegium, 1076-1077.

546 HAM 28i Flos filius.
        Clausula. ca.1250. 3 voices. Notre Dame school.
        Score parallels those of 2 related motets.

Flos filius, 282, 546, 1289.

Flours d'iver, 712.

Flow my tears, 451, 455.

547 HAM 94 FOGLIANO, Giacomo, 1468-1548.
        ⌐Ave Maria gratia plena⌐ Lauda. 4 voices.

Fol malin en son coeur, 668.

548 Scher 79 FOLZ, Hans, 16th cent.
        ⌐Kettenton⌐ Meisterlied. ca.1560.

Fons bonitatis, 882.

549 HAM 198 FONTANA, Giovanni Battista, d.1630.
        ⌐Sonata, violin & continuo, C major⌐

550 Hamb 87   ⌐Sonata, violin & continuo, G major⌐

For unto us a Child is born, 726.

Forqueray, 1306.

Forseulement, 1121.

Fortuna, 1433.

Fortuna d'un gran tempo, 806.

Fortuna, du scherzest, 509.

Fortz chausa es, 615.

Forza della virtù, 845.

551 Glea 47 Fowles in the frith.
        Gymel, conductus style. English, ca. 1270. 2 voices.

552 Scher 115 FRANCESCO da Milano, 1497-1543.
        ⌐Fantasia, lute⌐

553 Flor 61   ⌐Toccata, lute⌐

554 HAM 168 FRANCK, Melchior, 1580(ca.)-1639.
        ⌐Musicalischer Bergkreyen. So wünsch ich ihr⌐ Lied.
        4 voices.

555 Wolf 62   ⌐Newes teutsches musicalisches fröliches convivium.
        No.12⌐ In illo tempore. Quodlibet. 4 voices.

556 Wolf 63   ⌐Newes teutsches musicalisches fröliches convivium.
        No.13⌐ Zart schöne Jungfräulein. Tanzlied. 5 voices.

557 Starr 14 FRAUENLOB, Heinrich, d.1318.
        ⌐Ey ich sach in dem Trone⌐ Leich (lai) Minnelied.

558 Scher 21   [In der grünen Weise] Spruch. Minnelied.

559 OM 34   [Myn vroud ist gar czugangyn] Spruch, bar form. Minnelied.

Fraw, wilt du wissen, 982.

Freien ist kein Pferdekauf, 866.

560 Scher 196   FRESCOBALDI, Girolamo Alessandro, 1583-1643.
         [Fiori musicali. Canzona dopo l'epistola, C major] Organ.

561 SS 2c   [Fiori musicali. Kyrie cunctipotens] Organ.

562 MM 34   [Fiori musicali. Ricercar dopo il credo] Organ.
    Starr 100

563 Hamb 81   Toccata sexti toni, organ.

564 Flor 120   [Toccatas, keyboard instrument, book 1. Balletto secondo] With its Corrente.

565 HAM 192   [Toccatas, keyboard instrument, book 1. Partite sopra l'aria della Romanesca] Variations.

566 Flor 119   [Toccatas, keyboard instrument, book 2. Canzona terza]

567 HAM 194   [Toccatas, keyboard instrument, book 2. Canzona quarta]

568 Lern 65   [Toccatas, keyboard instrument, book 2. Toccata quinta]

569 HAM 193   [Toccatas, keyboard instrument, book 2. Toccata nona]

Toccate d'intavolatura di cimbalo et organo. see his [Toccatas, keyboard instrument]

Frèse nouvele, 1149.

Freundschaft, 32.

570 TEM 31   Fricassée.
         Quodlibet. 16th cent. 4 voices.

571 Scher 307   FRIEDRICH II, der Grosse, King of Prussia, 1712-1786.
         [Sonata, flute & continuo, no.22, G minor. Adagio]

572 Scher 289   FRITZSCH, J G A , supposed composer.
         [Lob des Schnupftabacks] Song with keyboard. ca.1747.

573 Flor 131   FROBERGER, Johann Jakob, 1616-1667.
    Hamb 86   [Suite, harpsichord, B minor]

574 HAM 216   [Suite, harpsichord, C major. Allemande] Lamento sopra la dolorosa perdita della Real Maestà di Ferdinando IV.

575 MM 35   [Suite, harpsichord, E minor]

576 Scher 205   [Suite, harpsichord, G minor]

577 HAM 217   [Toccata, organ, D minor]

Frölich wesen, 811.

578 TEM 14   FRONCIACO, fl.14th cent.
         [Kyrie trope] 4 voices.

Frühlingszeit, 859.

579 RR 24 FRYE, Walter, 15th cent.
⌈Ave regina⌉ Cantilena motet. 3 voices.

580 Scher 114 FUENLLANA, Miguel de, 16th cent.
⌈Orphenica lyra. De antequera sale el moro⌉ Romanze.
Voice and lute.

581 Flor 74 ⌈Paseábase el rey⌉ Song. Voice and lute.
     HAM 123

Fürchtet euch nicht, 1007.

582 HAM 2 Fuki no kyoku.
Voice and koto. Japanese.

Fundamentum organisandi, 1188-1190.

Funeste piaggi, 1209.

583 Scher 272 FUX, Johann Joseph, 1660-1741.
⌈Costanza e fortezza. Saprei morir⌉ Da capo aria,
act 2, scene 10. With instrumental ensemble. K.315.

584 Scher 271 ⌈Missa di San Carlo. Qui tollis⌉ Canon. 4 voices.
K.7.

585 Ein 21 GABRIELI, Andrea, 1510(ca.)-1586.
⌈Intonazione, organ, 2⁰ tono⌉

586 HAM 135 ⌈Intonazione, organ, 7⁰ tono⌉

587 HAM 136 ⌈Madrigale e ricercari. Ricercare, 12⁰ tono⌉ 4 instruments.

588 MM 21 ⌈Pour ung plaisir, keyboard⌉ From Canzoni alla france-
     Wolf 57 se... libro 4 or 5. MM 21 score shown parallel to
that of the polyphonic chanson setting by Crecquillon.

589 Scher 130 ⌈Psalmi Davidici. De profundis⌉ Motet. 6 voices.
From Psalm 130 (129).

590 Hamb 75b ⌈Susanne un jour, keyboard⌉ From Canzoni alla francese... libro 5. Score shown parallel to that of the
polyphonic chanson setting by Lassus.

591 Flor 81 ⌈Toccata, organ, 12⁰ tono⌉

592 Hamb 76 GABRIELI, Giovanni, 1557-1612.
⌈Canzoni et sonate per sonar con ogni sorte de instru-
menti. Canzona, 5 instruments, C major⌉

593 Lern 54 ⌈Canzoni per sonar a quattro. La spiritata⌉ 4 instruments.

594 Ein 19 ⌈Concerti, 6-16 parts. O magnum mysterium⌉ Motet.
     Hamb 47 2 4-part choirs.

595 Flor 101 ⌈Intonazioni, organ, 3⁰ e 4⁰ tono⌉

596 Lern 53 ⌈Sacrae symphoniae. Iam non dicam⌉ Motet. 2 4-part
choruses.

597 HAM 157 ⌈Sacrae symphoniae. In ecclesiis⌉ Motet. Solo voices,
double chorus, brass instruments, violin, and organ.

598	Nort3 13	⌐Sacrae symphoniae. Nunc dimittis⌐ Motet. Triple chorus: 5, 4, 5 voices.
599	Flor 102 HAM 173 Scher 148 Starr 63	⌐Sacrae symphoniae. Sonata pian' e forte⌐ 2 4-part instrumental groups.
600	Ein 28	GABRIELLI, Domenico, 1659-1690. ⌐Poiche ad Irene⌐ Chamber cantata. Voice and continuo.
601	Scher 228	⌐Ricercar, violoncello, D minor⌐
602	Ein 24	GAGLIANO, Marco da, d.1642. ⌐Dafne. Dunque ruvida scorza⌐ Aria.
603	Scher 175	⌐Dafne. Oimè, che vegg'io?⌐ Chorus and recitative, with instrumental ensemble.
604	Scher 112	Gagliarda veneziana. ca.1551. Keyboard.
605	Glea 12 Min 13 OM 20	Gaite de la tor. Trouvère aube. ca.1200.
		Galante, 380.
606	Scher 91	Galliarde. Keyboard. (Attaingnant, 1530).
		Gallus, Jacobus, see HANDL, Jacob
607	HAM 285	GALUPPI, Baldassare, called Il Buranello, 1706-1785. ⌐Il filosofo di campagna. Da me non speri⌐ Aria with instrumental ensemble.
608	Flor 168	⌐Il filosofo di campagna. La mia region è questa⌐ Aria from act 1, scene 3. With instrumental ensemble.
609	HAM 119	GANASSI, Silvestro, fl.1535. ⌐Regola Rubertina. Selections⌐ Libro 1, no.1 and Libro 2, no.2. Ricercari. Viola da gamba.
		Gardana, 995.
		Gassenhawer, 1097.
610	Hamb 56	GASTOLDI, Giovanni Giacomo, d.1622. ⌐A lieta vita⌐ Balletto. 5 voices.
611	HAM 158	⌐L'acceso⌐ Balletto. 5 voices.
612	Flor 100	⌐Lo schernito⌐ Balletto. 5 voices.
613	Ein 20	⌐Speme amorosa⌐ Balletto. 5 voices.
614	Wolf 47	⌐Viver lieto voglio⌐ Balletto. 5 voices.
615	OM 15	GAUCELM, Faidit, ca.1170-1205. ⌐Fortz chausa es⌐ Troubadour planh in vers form.
		Gaude gloriosa, 1233.
		Gaude Maria, 949.

616   Nort3 1   Gaudeamus omnes.
                       Introit. Gregorian chant.

617   TEM 3   Gaudete populi.
                       Antiphon of the Mass for Easter. Mozarabic chant.

                    Gaulcem. see GAUCELM

618   Scher 215b GAULTIER, Denis, 1600(ca.)-1672.
                       ⌈La rhétorique des dieux. La consolation aux amis du
                       Sr. Lenclos⌉ Lute.

619   HAM 211   ⌈La rhétorique des dieux. Mode sous-ionien⌉ Lute
                       dance.

620   TEM 39   ⌈La rhétorique des dieux. Tombeau de Mademoiselle
                       Gaultier⌉ Lute. Tablature, with transcription for
                       keyboard.

621   Scher 215a   ⌈La rhétorique des dieux. Tombeau des Mons. de Lenclos⌉
                       Lute.

                    Geborn ist der Emanuel, 1262.

                    Gehe, guter Peter, 768.

                    Geistliche Chormusik, 1408.

                    Geistliche Oden und Lieder, 97.

                    Gelobet seist du, 127, 236, 1159, 1389, 1396, 1596.

622   OM 60   Gemma florens militiae.
                       Isorhythmic motet. Cypriot-French, ca.1400. 4 voices.
                       Polytext: Gemma florens; Haec est dies; textless tenor
                       and contratenor.

623   Amb 32   GENET, Elzéar, called Carpentras, 1470(ca.)-1548.
                       ⌈Lamentationes Hieremiae Prophetae. Selections⌉ 7 ex-
                       cerpts. 3-4 equal voices.

624   HAM 137   GERVAISE, Claude, 16th cent.
                       ⌈Danceries, livre 2. La volunté⌉ Basse danse. 4 in-
                       struments.

625   HAM 137   ⌈Danceries, livre 3. Allemande⌉ 4 instruments.

626   HAM 137   ⌈Danceries, livre 6. Pavane d'Angleterre avec sa
      Min 55   gaillarde⌉ 5 instruments.

                    Gesangweise, 1345.

                    Gespräch einer Jungfrauen, 33.

627   Scher 167   GESUALDO, Carlo, principe di Venosa, 1560(ca.)-1613.
                       ⌈Madrigals, 5 voices, book 5. Dolcissima mia vita⌉

628   Flor 105   ⌈Madrigals, 5 voices, book 5. Itene, or miei sospiri⌉

629   Lern 60   ⌈Madrigals, 5 voices, book 5. Mercè grido piangendo⌉

630   HAM 161   ⌈Madrigals, 5 voices, book 6. Io pur respiro⌉

631   Starr 37   ⌈Madrigals, 5 voices, book 6. Moro lasso⌉
      TEM 33

632   Hamb 48c   ⌈Madrigals, 5 voices, book 6. Resta di darmi noia⌉

633 Glea 100   GHIRARDELLO da Firenze, fl.1375.
     HAM 52   ⌐Tosto che l'alba⌐ Caccia. 3 voices, one a free tenor.
     Hamb 27
     Starr 25

634 Amb 26   GHISELIN, Johannes, fl.1491-1535.
                     ⌐La Alfonsina⌐ Chanson. 3 voices.

635 Wolf 55   GHRO, Johann.
                     ⌐Neue auserlesene Padovanen und Galliarden (1604)
                     Padovana I⌐ 4 instruments.

                 Giasone, 308.

636 Lern 58   GIBBONS, Orlando, 1583-1625.
                     ⌐Behold thou hast made my days⌐ Anthem. 5 voices.

637 TEM 36   ⌐In nomine, 4 viols⌐

638 Flor 118   ⌐Madrigals and motets, set 1. The silver swan⌐ Madri-
     Nort 5   gal. 5 voices.
     Starr 45

639 HAM 171   ⌐O Lord, increase my faith⌐ Anthem. 4 voices.

640 HAM 179   ⌐Pavane Lord Salisbury, harpsichord⌐

641 HAM 172   ⌐This is the record of John⌐ Verse anthem. Tenor,
                     chorus, and 4 viols.

642 Wolf 32   GINTZLER, Simon, fl.1547.
                     ⌐Intabolatura de lauto (1547) Recercar sexto⌐
                     Preambel (published 1552; a slightly altered version of
                     the 1547 recercar).

                 Gioite al canto mio, 1210.

                 Giosuè, 202.

643 TEM 16   GIOVANNI da Cascia, fl.1329-1351.
                     ⌐Con brachi assai⌐ Caccia. 3 voices.

644 Ein 10   ⌐Io son un pellegrin⌐ Ballata. 2 voices.
     HAM 51
     Hamb 26

645 HAM 50   ⌐Nel mezzo a sei paon⌐ Madrigal. 2 voices.

646 Scher 22   ⌐O tu cara scienzia mia⌐ Madrigal. 2 voices.

                 Giulio Cesare, 722.

                 Giunta vaga biltà, 894.

                 Giustino, 938.

                 Gläut zu Speyer, 1434.

                 Gleichwie ein kleines Vögelein, 1398.

647 RR 141b   Glogauer Liederbuch.
                     Es leit ein Schloss in Österreich. 3 voices.

648 HAM 83a   Glogauer Liederbuch.
                     Instrumental piece. 3 parts.

649   HAM 83b   Glogauer Liederbuch.
        Hamb 45   Der neue Bauernschwanz.   Dance.   3 instruments.

650   HAM 82   Glogauer Liederbuch.
                    O rosa bella.   Quodlibet.   3 voices.

651   Scher 50   Glogauer Liederbuch.
                    Das yeger horn.   ca.1480.   3 instruments.

                 Gloria, 652, 670, 1057, 1194.

652   Lern 3   Gloria IX.
                    Gregorian chant.

653   Flor 19   Gloria in cielo.
                    Lauda, 13th cent.

654   Glea 22   Gloria in cielo.
        HAM 21a   Lauda (virelai)   14th cent.   1 voice.
        Hamb 11

655   HAM 57b   Gloria in excelsis.
                    14th cent.   3 voices.   Fauxbourdon style.   Worcester
                    school.

                 Gloriosae virginis Mariae, 1258.

                 Godi l'amabile, 671.

                 Godi, turba mortal, 301.

656   RMA 63   GODRIC, Saint, d.1170.
                    ⌐Crist and Sainte Marie⌐   Song.   1 voice.

657   HAM 23a   ⌐Sainte Marie virgine⌐   English song.   1 voice.

658   Lern 19   ⌐Sainte Nicholaes, godes druth⌐   English religious song.
                    1 voice.

                 Goe from my window, 1081.

659   Scher 300   GÖRNER, Johann Valentin, 1702-1762.
                    ⌐Neue Oden und Lieder.   An den Schlaf⌐   Voice with key-
                    board.

                 Götter, übt Barmherzigkeit, 841.

660   Scher 102   GOMBERT, Nicolas, fl.1520-1552.
                    ⌐Missa, Media vita.   Agnus Dei II⌐   6 voices.

661   Amb 33   ⌐Motets, 4 voices, book 1.   Ave regina coelorum⌐

662   HAM 114   ⌐Motets, 4 voices, book 1.   Super flumina Babylonis⌐

663   RR 172   GOMOŁKA, Mikołaj, fl.1535-1591.
                    ⌐Melodye na psałtera polski.   Psalm 25⌐   4 voices.

                 Gott sei gelobet, 1156, 1318.

664   Hamb 63   GOUDIMEL, Claude, d.1572.
                    ⌐Psaumes de David, no.8⌐   O nostre Dieu.   4 voices.

665   TEM 25-26   ⌐Psaumes de David, no.23⌐   Mon Dieu me paist sous sa.
                    2 4-part settings in parallel score.   From the French
                    Psalters of 1564 and 1565.

666 HAM 126a ⌐Psaumes de David, no.35¬ Deba contre mes debateurs.
4 voices.

667 Scher 142 ⌐Psaumes de David, no.42¬ Ainsi quón oit le cerf
bruire. 4 voices.

668 Flor 78 ⌐Psaumes de David, no.53¬ Le fol malin en son coeur.
4 voices.

669 RR 116 ⌐Psaumes de David, no.134¬ Or sus, serviteurs.
4 voices.

Gram piant' agli ochi, 895.

Gran dereit', 43.

Grates nunc omnes, 869.

670 OM 63 GRATIOSUS de Padua, fl.ca.1500.
⌐Gloria¬ Isolated mass movement. 3 voices.

Gratissima virginis, 1233.

671 HAM 282 GRAUN, Karl Heinrich, 1704-1759.
⌐Montezuma. Godi l'amabile¬ Cavatina. Voice with instrumental ensemble.

672 Scher 308 ⌐Der Tod Jesu. Christus hat uns ein Vorbild gelassen¬
Choral fugue. 4 voices with instrumental ensemble.

Graziani, 1576.

673 Hamb 51 GREAVES, Thomas, fl.1604.
⌐Songes of sundrie kindes. Madrigals, 5 part. Come
away sweet love¬ Ballett.

674 HAM 279 GREENE, Maurice, 1696?-1755.
⌐Acquaint thyself with God. Selections¬ Anthem. Sec-
tion for tenor solo with organ.

675 Scher 206 GREFFLINGER, Georg, 17th cent.
⌐Seladons weltliche Lieder. No.3¬ Hylas wil kein weib
haben. First line: Schweiget mir vom Weibernehmen.
Voice with continuo.

676 OM 5 Gregorian plainsong modes.
The tenor, final, and ambitus of each mode in authentic
and plagal form.

677 Amb 42 GREITER, Mathias.
⌐Ich stund an einem Morgen¬ Lied. 4 voices.

678 Wolf 10 GRENON, Nicolas, d.1456.
⌐Je ne requier de ma dame¬ Ballade. 3 voices.

679 Scher 263 GRIGNY, Nicolas de, 1672-1703.
⌐Livre d'orgue. Fugue, E major¬

Grillo, 419.

Griselda, 357, 1369-1370.

Guardame las vacas, 1544.

Guardian angels, 740.

Gülden Ton, 1346.

680	HAM 139	GUERRERO, Francisco, 1527-1599. [Salve regina] Antiphon B.M.V. (motet) 4 solo voices and chorus.
681	Glea 26	GUIDO d'Arezzo, 990(ca.)-1050. [Micrologus. Selections.] Examples of organum.
		GUIDO d'Arezzo. see also Ut queant laxis
682	Flor 68b	Guido e Pellegrino. Dialogued lauda. ca.1550. 3 voices.
683	OM 105	GUILIELMUS Monachus, 15th cent. [Falla con misuras] Basse danse. 2 instruments.
684	Scher 33	[Piece, 3 instruments] Upper parts in gymel.
685	Glea 10 HAM 19f Lern 15	GUILLAUME d'Amiens, 13th cent. [C'est la fin] Trouvère virelai.
686	Flor 16a HAM 19g	[E, dame jolie] Trouvère virelai.
687	HAM 19h	[Pour mon cuer] Trouvère rotrouenge.
688	Glea 9 Lern 14	[Prendés i garde] Trouvère rondeau.
689	HAM 19e	[Vos n'aler] Trouvère rondeau.
690	HAM 46a Hamb 24	GUILLAUME de Machaut, d.1377. [Comment qu'a moy] Virelai. 1 voice.
691	Glea 80	[Dame, mon cuer] Virelai. 2 voices.
692	Glea 88	[De bon espoir] Motet. 3 voices. Polytext: De bon espoir; Puis que la douce; Speravi.
693	Ein 11	[De toutes flours] Ballade. 3 voices and instruments.
694	RMA 105	[Douce dame jolie] Virelai. 1 voice.
695	OM 69	[J'aim la flour] Trouvère lai.
696	HAM 45 Hamb 23	[Je puis trop bien] Ballade. 3 voices.
697	Scher 26a	[Ma chiere dame] Ballade. 3 voices.
698	Flor 33 Glea 81 RMA 107 Starr 23	[Ma fin est mon commencement] Rondeau. 3 voices.
699	Glea 85	[Mes esperis se combat] Ballade. 3 voices.
700	SS 6b	[La Messe de Nostre Dame. Selections] Agnus Dei and Ita missa est. 4 voices.
701	Flor 32b Glea 97 MM 13	[La Messe de Nostre Dame. Agnus Dei I] 4 voices.
702	Nort3 3 Starr 20	[La Messe de Nostre Dame. Kyrie] 4 voices.

703	HAM 46b	⌐Plus dure que un dyamant⌐ Virelai. 2 voices.
704	Lern 27	⌐Qui es promesses⌐ Motet. 3 voices. Polytext: Qui es promesses; Ha! fortune; Et non est qui adjuvet.
705	HAM 44 Hamb 22	⌐S'il estoit nulz⌐ Isorhythmic motet. 3 voices. Polytext: S'il estoit nulz; S'amours tous amans; Et gaudebit cor vestrum.
706	OM 70	⌐Sans cuer⌐ Canonic ballade. 3 voices. Polytext: Sans cuer; Amis, dolens; Dame, par vous.
707	OM 68 SS 19 Scher 26b	⌐Se je souspir⌐ Virelai. 2 voices.
708	OM 71	⌐Tant doulcement⌐ Rondeau. 4 voices.
709	Wolf 5	⌐Ton corps qui de bien amer⌐ Motet. 3 voices. Polytext: Ton corps...; De souspirant cuer; Suspiro.
710	Scher 27	⌐Trop plus est belle⌐ Motet. 3 voices. Polytext: Trop plus; Biauté parée de valour; Je ne suis mie certains.
711	HAM 19i	GUILLAUME le Vinier, 1190(ca.)-1245. ⌐Espris d'ire⌐ Trouvère lai.
712	OM 21	⌐La flours d'iver⌐ Trouvère song.
713	OM 24	GUILLEBERT de Berneville, 13th cent. ⌐Cuidoient li losengier⌐ Trouvère rotrouenge.
714	OM 19	GUIOT de Dijon, 12th cent. ⌐Chanterai por mon coraige⌐ Trouvère chanson de Croisade, 1189.
715	HAM 18c RMA 50	GUIRAUT de Bornelh, ca.1140-1220. ⌐Reis glorios⌐ Troubadour alba. HAM gives 3 rhythmic interpretations.
716	Flor 15c	GUIRAUT Riquier, ca.1230-1300. ⌐Tant mes plazens⌐ Troubadour song.
		Gulielmus. see GUILIELMUS Monachus
		Gut Singer und ein Organist, 932.
717	RR 169	H , M ⌐Bog wieczny a wszechmocny⌐ Sacred song. Polish, 16th cent. 4 voices.
		Ha! fortune, 704.
718	Glea 49 HAM 39	Hac in anni janua. Conductus. English, 13th cent. 3 voices.
		Haec dies. see also Hec dies
719	HAM 12	Haec dies. Gradual. Gregorian chant.
		Haec dies, 719, 950, 1215.
		Haec est dies, 622.
		Haec est sancta solemnitas, 1107.

720	MM 43	HÄNDEL, Georg Friedrich, 1685-1759. ⌐Concerto grosso, C major. Allegro¬ "Alexanderfest" concerto. 1st movement. B.105.
721	Flor 161	⌐Duets, voices & harpsichord. No.12, Tanti strali al sen. Part 1¬ B.36, no.11.
722	Nort3 21	⌐Giulio Cesare. Piangerò¬ Soprano aria. With instrumental ensemble. B.70.
723	Starr 190	⌐Israel in Egypt. Who is like unto Thee¬ Chorus with orchestra. B.117.
724	Nort 8 Nort3 22	⌐Messiah. Comfort ye my people¬ Tenor aria. No.2 of the oratorio. B.130.
725	Nort 8 Nort3 22	⌐Messiah. Ev'ry valley¬ Tenor aria. No.3 of the oratorio. B.130.
726	Nort 8 Nort3 22	⌐Messiah. For unto us a Child is born¬ Chorus. No.12 of the oratorio. 4 voices. B.130.
727	Nort 8 Nort3 22	⌐Messiah. Hallelujah¬ Chorus. No.44 of the oratorio. 4 voices. B.130.
728	Nort 8	⌐Messiah. He was despised¬ Alto aria. No.23 of the oratorio. B.130.
729	Nort 3 22	⌐Messiah. Overture¬ Sinfonia. B.130.
730	MM 44	⌐Rinaldo. Selections¬ Recitative (Al valor del mio brando), Sinfonia, and Aria (Cara sposa). B.37.
731	Starr 194	⌐Rinaldo. Ogni indugio d'un amante¬ Aria. With instrumental ensemble. B.37.
732	Scher 278	⌐Rinaldo. Overture¬ Strings and continuo. B.37.
733	SS 33	⌐Rodelinda. Act 1. Selections¬ Sinfonia, recitatives, and aria; and aria and recitative from scene 7. B.73.
734	MM 45	⌐Solomon. Draw the tear from hopeless love¬ Chorus. B.142.
735	Lern 81	⌐Solomon. May no rash intruder¬ Chorus. B.142.
736	SS 54	⌐Sonatas, op.1. No.11, F major¬ Recorder and continuo. B.67, no.11.
737	Scher 279	⌐Suites, harpsichord, 1st collection. No.8, F minor. Prelude¬ B.60, no.8.
738	Lern 80	⌐Tolomeo. Che più si tarda omai¬ Recitative and aria. With instrumental ensemble. B.81.
739	Starr 188	⌐Trio-sonata, oboes & continuo, no.1, G minor¬ B.1, no.1.
740	Scher 280	⌐Triumph of time and truth. Guardian angels¬ Da capo aria from the end of the oratorio. Soprano with instrumental ensemble. B.153.

Hallelujah chorus, 727.

741 HAM 213   HAMMERSCHMIDT, Andreas, 1612-1675.
[Dialogi oder Gespräche zwischen Gott und einer gläubigen Seelen, Teil 1. No.20] Wende Dich Herr. Alto and bass with trombone and continuo.

742 Scher 194   [Weltliche Oden, Teil 1. No.13] Kusslied. Voice and continuo.

Handel, GF see HÄNDEL, GF

743 Amb 60a   HANDL, Jacob, known as Gallus, 1550-1591.
[Cantiones sacrae, tom.I. No.8] Jerusalem gaude gaudio magno. Motet. 6 voices.

744 Amb 60b   [Cantiones sacrae, tom.I. No.12] Laetentur coeli et exultet. Motet. 6 voices.

745 HAM 156   [Ecce quomodo moritur] Responsorium. Motet. 4 voices.
     Scher 131

746 Min 37   [Hodie Christus natus est] Motet. 6 voices. From his Opus musicum, v.1.

Hark, all ye lovely saints, 1612.

Hark Harry, 496.

Harmonische Freude musikalischer Freunde, 509-510.

747 HAM 281   HASSE, Johann Adolf, 1699-1783.
[La conversione di Sant' Agostino. Ma giunge appunto]

748 Flor 165   [La conversione di Sant' Agostino. Non abbandona mai Iddio] Da capo aria (first part).

749 Scher 310   [Requiem, C minor. Lacrymosa] Soloists, chorus, and orchestra.

750 HAM 164   HASSLER, Hans Leo, 1564-1612.
[Cantiones sacrae. No.13] Quia vidisti me Thoma. Motet. 4 voices.

751 TEM 28   [Cantiones sacrae. No.44] Laudate Dominum. Motet. 2 4-part choirs.

752 Amb 59   [Kirchengesänge. Herzlich lieb hab ich dich] 2 4-part choirs.

753 Flor 108   [Lustgarten neuer teutscher Gesäng. No.15] All Lust und Freud. 4 voices.

754 Hamb 60a   [Lustgarten neuer teutscher Gesäng. No.24] Mein G'müth ist mir verwirret. 5 voices.

755 Scher 152   [Lustgarten neuer teutscher Gesäng. No.29] Ach, süsse Seel'. 6 voices.

756 Scher 153   [Lustgarten neuer teutscher Gesäng. No.41] Intrada. 6 instruments.

757 HAM 165   [Neue teutsche Gesäng. No.15] Ach Schatz ich thu dir klagen. 5 voices.

758 HAM 4   Hāu ājyadohamma.
                   Hindu sâman (chant), ca.1000 BC. Ancient notation, and
                   transcription from a modern recording.

759 Scher 155 HAUSSMANN, Valentin, fl.1588-1611.
                   ⌐Neue Paduane und Galliarde (1604) Pavane and galliard⌐
                   5 instruments.

760 Wolf 54   ⌐Polnische und andere Tänze (1603) Dance⌐ 5 instru-
                   ments.

                Haut honor d'un commandement, 1522.

                Hé Diex! quant verrai, 17.

                He parthenos semeron, 1330.

                He was despised, 728.

                Hear the voice and prayer, 1484.

                Hec dies. see also Haec dies

761 HAM 30   Hec dies.
                   Clausula. 2 voices. Notre Dame school.

762 Flor 24   Hec dies.
     HAM 29   Organum. ca.1175. 2 voices. Notre Dame school.
     Hamb 16

763 HAM 31   Hec dies.
     Hamb 17   Organum. ca.1200. 3 voices. Notre Dame school.

                Hec dies, 409, 761-763, 783, 790, 1290.

                Hei mihi infelix Magdalena, 335.

                Heiligen drei Könige Aufzug, 1102.

                Heinrich von Meissen. see FRAUENLOB, Heinrich

                Hélas! il n'est mais, 11.

764 Hamb 40a   HELLINCK, Lupus, d.1541.
                   ⌐Panis quem ego dabo. Part 1⌐. Motet. 4 voices.

                Henrico Leone, 1460.

765 RMA 25   HERMANNUS Contractus, 1013-1054.
                   ⌐Alma redemptoris mater⌐ Antiphon.

766 Scher 7   ⌐Ter terni sunt modi⌐ Versus ad discernendum cantum.
                   1 voice. From his exercises to learn intervals.

767 OM 12   Herod (Liturgical drama)
                   From the Fleury play-book, 12th cent.

                Herr hat seinen Engeln, 198.

                Herr ist meine Stärke, 1423.

                Herr, nun lässest du deinen Diener, 179.

                Herr, wie Du willst, 199.

                Herzlich lieb hab ich dich, 752.

                Hey, Robyn, 374.

Hey, Trola, 1241.

Heylsame Geburth und Menschwerdung unsers Herrn, 1007.

Hic est beatissimus, 1086.

Hic verus Dei, 402.

Hilff Herr, 1467.

768 Scher 309b HILLER, Johann Adam, 1728-1804.
⌐Der Erntekranz. Gehe, guter Peter⌐ Aria from the
Singspiel. With keyboard.

769 Flor 175 ⌐Die Jagd. Du warst zwar sonst ein gutes Kind⌐ Aria
from the Singspiel.

770 HAM 301 ⌐Lisuart und Dariolette. Bald die Blonde⌐ Aria from
the Singspiel.

771 Wolf 66 HILTON, John, 1599-1657.
⌐Leave off, sad Philomel⌐ Air. 3 voices. Ayres or
fa-las (1627), no.11.

Himmel, du weisst meine Plagen, 510.

Historia von der Auferstehung Jesu Christi, 1409.

Hither, dear husband, 1197.

772 Wolf 2 Hoc est pulcrum evangelium.
Organum (responsory) 15th cent. 3 voices.

Hodie cantandus est, 1534.

Hodie Christus natus est, 746.

773 OM 8 Hodie nobis caelorum Rex.
1st responsory at Matins on Christmas Day. Gregorian
chant.

Hör Menschenkind, 947.

Hoffe noch, 842.

Hoffheimer, Paulus. see HOFHAIMER, Paul

774 Amb 37a HOFHAIMER, Paul, 1459-1537.
⌐Ach lieb mit leid⌐ Lied. 4 voices.

775 Amb 37b ⌐Ich hab heimlich ergeben mich⌐ Lied. 4 voices.

776 Amb 37c ⌐Mein's traurens ist⌐ Lied. 4 voices.
HAM 93

777 Lern 41 ⌐Nach willen dein⌐ Lied. 4 voices.

778 RR 148 ⌐Salve regina, organ. O clemens⌐

779 Wolf 25 ⌐Unschuldiger Ritter⌐ 4 instruments.

Holder Zephyr, 845.

Holdseliger meins Hertzen Trost, 1598.

780   HAM 66a   Homme armé.
     Hamb 30   French melody, 15th cent.
     Nort3 8
     RR 18
     Starr 28

Homme armé, 423-424, 476-477, 780, 905, 1138-1139.

781   OM 43   Homo quo vigeas.
         Clausula-motet. ca.1170. 3 voices. Polytext: Homo
         quo vigeas; Homo quo vigeas; Et gaudebit. Notre Dame
         school.

Hor per vegnir, 1545.

Hora decima, 1229.

Hora e di Maggio, 807.

Hoson zes phainou, 1428.

782   Scher 31   HUBERTUS de Salinis, fl.1400.
         ⌈Salve regina⌉ Motet. 3 voices.

Hüssler, Johann. see WECK, Hans

Hugo de Lantins. see LANTINS, Hugo de

783   HAM 32a   Huic main.
         Motet. 13th cent. 2 voices. Polytext: Huic main; Hec
         dies. Incomplete.

Huius chori, 994.

784   HAM 242   HUMFREY, Pelham, 1647-1674.
         ⌈O Lord, my God⌉ Verse anthem. Voice and chorus with
         organ.

Humphrey, Pelham. see HUMFREY, Pelham

Hylas wil kein weib haben, 675.

Hymn to Apollo, 840.

Hymn to Nemesis, 1022.

Hymn to St. Magnus, 1101.

Hymn to the muse, 1020.

Hymn to the sun, 1021.

785   HAM 8b   Hymnoumen ton sotera.
         Hymn from the Octoechos. Byzantine chant, 13th cent.

Hymnum cantemus, 294.

786   OM 44   Hypocritae, pseudopontifices.
         Motet. French, ca.1210. 3 voices. Polytext: Hypocri-
         tae; Velut stellae firmamenti; Et gaudebit.

I call you all, 1282.

I care not for these ladies, 278.

I gave her cakes, 1280.

I have been a foster, 359.

I will love Thee, O Lord, 1281.

Iam non dicam, 596.

Ich armer Mann, 910.

Ich bin ein guter Hirt, 112.

Ich dank dir, lieber Herre, 1263.

Ich hab heimlich ergeben mich, 775.

Ich hab mich redlich ghalten, 1402.

Ich heb' mein' Augen sehnlich auf, 1417.

Ich sach einsmals, 1402.

Ich stieg auf einen Birnenbaum, 1340.

Ich stund an einem Morgen, 677.

Ich warne dich, 1628.

Ich will zu Land ausreiten, 1454.

Ihr bleibet nicht Bestand verpflicht, 860.

Il covient qu'en la chandoile, 1221.

Il faut passer, 962.

787 HAM 84a-b   ILEBORGH von Stendal, Adam, 15th cent.
      [Tablature (1448) Selections] Organ preludes, no.1
      in G and no.4 super D, A, F et G.

Illumina oculos, 808.

Im Maien hört man die Hanen kreen, 1435.

In der grünen Weise, 558.

In dulci jubilo, 128, 237.

In ecclesiis, 597.

788 OM 7   In exitu Israel.
      Psalm, with antiphon Deus autem noster. 5th psalm at
      Vespers on Sundays. Gregorian chant, tonus peregrinus.

In festis duplicibus, 1000-1001.

In hora ultima, 911.

In illo tempore, 555, 1072.

In manus tuas, 1482.

In nomine, 637, 1512.

789 Scher 8   In resurrectione (Liturgical drama)
      ca.1100. Solo voice and unison chorus.

790 HAM 32e   In seculum.
      Motet. Hocket. 13th cent. 3 instruments. Based on
      Hec dies.

In seculum, 790-791, 827, 1528.

791 Flor 27   In seculum artifex.
     RMA 90   Motet. 13th cent. 3 voices. Polytext: In seculum
                     artifex; In seculum, supra mulieres; In seculum.

792 Lern 25   In seculum d'amiens longum.
                     Instrumental motet. Hocket. 13th cent. 3 instruments.

793 TEM 11   In seculum longum.
                     Instrumental motet. Hocket. 13th cent. 3 instru-
                     ments. Score includes a 4th, vocal, part, later added
                     to form the 4-voiced motet Je n'amerai autre (q.v.).

794 Glea 58   In seculum viellatoris.
     Scher 20   Motet. French, 13th cent. 3 instruments.

                 In te Domine, 420.

795 RMA 123   In te Domine speravi.
                     English discant. 13th cent. 3 voices.

                 In un boschetto, 990.

                 In vasto mare infido, 1499.

                 Incoronazione di Poppea, 1041.

                 Indes galantes, 1302.

                 Indissolubilis amicitia, 1077.

796 TEM 5   Infantem vidimus (Liturgical drama)
                     Gregorian chant, 11th-12th cent. Also known as The
                     play of the three kings.

                 Inganni felici, 1371.

797 Flor 92   INGEGNERI, Marco Antonio, 1545(ca.)-1592.
     Wolf 41   ⌈Responsoria hebdomadae sanctae. Jerusalem surge⌉
                     Motet. 4 voices.

798 OM 106   Ingrata.
                     Ballo. Italian, 15th cent. 1 instrument.

                 Innsbruck, ich muss dich lassen, 809.

                 Integer vitae, 1023.

799 OM 27   Intellecto divino.
                     Lauda. Early 14th cent. Mensural reconstruction with
                     unmeasured transcription underlaid.

                 Introitus in Dominica, 513.

                 Io che c'alti sospir, 1207.

                 Io lo vedo, 1338.

                 Io moro, 309-310.

                 Io parto, 266.

                 Io piango et ella il volto, 987.

                 Io piango Filli, 302.

                 Io pur respiro, 630.

                 Io son ferito, 991.

Io son l'ocello che non pò volare, 1525.

Io son un pellegrin, 644.

800 Glea 23   Is milde lomb.
        English song (lai segment) 13th cent. 1 voice.

801 Amb 41b-d   ISAAC, Heinrich, 1450(ca.)-1517.
        [Works, vocal. Selections] 3 weltliche Lieder.
        3-5 voices. Without text.

802 Flor 53   [Canzona, 3 instruments]

803 HAM 88   [Canzona, 4 instruments]

804 Amb 40   [Choralis Constantinus, book 2. No.1] Puer natus est
        nobis. Introitus de nativitate Jesu Christi. 4 voices.
        2 settings.

805 Amb 39a   [Christus filius Dei] Motet. 6 voices. Auf das Ri-
        tualmotiv Virgo prudentissima. Includes the chant.

806 Amb 41a   [Donna di dentro] Quodlibet. 4 voices. Polytext:
        Donna di dentro; Fortuna d'un gran tempo.

807 Min 45   [Hora e di Maggio] Calendimaggio canzon.

808 Amb 38   [Illumina oculos] Motet. 3 equal voices.

809 Flor 54   [Innsbruck, ich muss dich lassen] Song. 4 voices.

810 Scher 56   [La Martinella] Canzona. Organ or 3 instruments.

811 Scher 55   [Missa, Frölich wesen, Kyrie] 4 voices.

812 RR 145   [Missa paschalis. Osanna] 5 voices.

813 Amb 39b   [Virgo prudentissima] Motet. 4 voices.

814 HAM 87   [Zwischen Berg und tiefem Tal] Song. 4 voices.
    Hamb 36
    Starr 33

Israel in Egypt, 723.

Iste confessor, 470.

Ite caldi sospiri, 213.

Itene, or miei sospiri, 628.

J'aim la flour, 695.

Ja nus hons pris, 1324.

815 OM 76   JACOPO da Bologna, 14th cent.
        [Aquila altera] Madrigal with ritornello. 3 voices.
        Polytext: Aquila altera; Creatura gentile; Uccel di
        Dio.

816 OM 85   [Aquila altera; arr.] 2 instruments. Italian, early
        15th cent. Anonymous.

817 Flor 35   [Di novo è giunt' un cavalier errante] Madrigal.
    RMA 112   2 voices.

818 Glea 99   [Fenice fu] Madrigal. 2 voices.
    Lern 28

819   HAM 49   [Non al suo amante]   Madrigal.   2 voices.
      Hamb 25

820   Scher 117   JACOTIN, 1445(ca.)-1529.
                  [Je suis déshéritée]   Chanson.   3 voices.

            Jagd, 769.

821   Starr 35   JANEQUIN, Clément, ca.1475-1560.
                  [A ce joly moys]   Chanson.   4 voices.

822   HAM 107   [Le chant de l'alouette]   Chanson.   4 voices.
      Hamb 49

823   Flor 60   [Le chant des oyseaux]   Polyphonic chanson.   4 voices.
                  Incomplete.

824   Scher 67   JAPART, Jean, fl.1500.
                  [Nenciozza mia]   Canzona.   4 instruments.

825   HAM 35   Je cuidoie.
                  Motet.   13th cent.   3 voices.   Polytext: Je cuidoie;
                  Se j'ai; Solem.

826   Starr 13   Je la truis.
                  Trouvère virelai.   ca.13th cent.

            Je la truis, 826, 1519.

            Je languis, 1271.

            Je m'en vois, 229.

827   Glea 70   Je n'amerai autre.
      TEM 12   Motet.   Hocket.   13th cent.   4 voices.   Polytext: Je
                  n'amerai autre; In seculum.   The three lower voices are
                  also the score to the instrumental motet In seculum
                  longum (q.v.).

            Je nay deul, 1133.

            Je ne l'ose dire, 321.

            Je ne requier de ma dame, 678.

            Je ne suis mie certains, 710.

            Je puis trop bien, 696.

            Je sey bien dire, 422.

            Je suis déshéritée, 269, 820.

828   Flor 34   Je vous salue.
                  Chanson.   14th cent.   3 voices.

829   Glea 10   JEHANNOT de l'Escurel, d.1303.
                  [Amours, cent mille]   Trouvère ballade.   Voice with
                  chorus.

            Jephte, 293-295.

            Jerusalem gaude gaudio magno, 743.

            Jerusalem surge, 797.

            Jesaia dem Propheten, 971.

830	Lern 17	Jesu Christo glorioso.
		Lauda. 1 voice.
831	Glea 48	Jesu Cristes milde moder.
		Gymel, conductus style. English, ca.1270. 2 voices.

Jesu, der du meine Seele, 113.

Jesus redemptor omnium, 1568.

Jesus tot, 952.

Jeu de Robin et de Marion, 12-14.

Jeunes zéphirs, 332.

Johannes Damaskenos. see JOHN of Damascus

Johannes de Florentia. see GIOVANNI da Cascia

Johannespassion, 114.

832	Scher VI	JOHN of Damascus, ca.690-750.
		⌜Engkainizesthe adelphoi⌝ Byzantine chant. From the hymns of the Sticherarion for September: for the consecration feast of the Resurrection Chruch.
833	HAM 299	JOMMELLI, Nicolò, 1714-1774.
		⌜Victimae paschali laudes. Mors e vita⌝ Motet. 6 solo voices with organ.

Jonas, 296.

Josquin des Près. see DEPRÈS, Josquin

Jouissance vous donneray, 1444.

Jour s'endort, 471.

834	RMA 34	Jubilate Deo.
		Offertory. Gregorian chant.

Jubilate Deo, 195, 834.

835	RMA 19	Jubilate Domino.
		Offertory. Ambrosian chant.

Jubilemus salvatori, 19.

Juden Tanz, 1095.

Judicium Salomonis, 297.

Justus ut palma, 58.

836	Glea 1	Kadosh, kadosh, kadosh.
		Hebrew chant. Sephardic.

Kalenda maya, 1295.

837	Scher 138	KARGEL, Sixt, late 16th cent.
		⌜Fantasia, lute⌝
838	RMA 10	KASIA, 9th cent.
		⌜Augoustou monarkhesantos⌝ Byzantine sticheron in sequence form.
839	RMA 8	Katal hwa yalude.
		Ancient Syrian hymn (sugyāthā).

840 HAM 7a Kechlyth', Helikona bathydendron hai lachete.
   Scher II   Hymn to Apollo. Greek, ca.150 BC. Unison voices.

841 Lern 79 KEISER, Reinhard, 1674-1739.
        ⌐Croesus. Götter, übt Barmherzigkeit¬ Aria, act 3,
        scene 1. With instrumental ensemble.

842 TEM 46   ⌐Croesus. Hoffe noch¬ Aria from act 1, scene 2. With
        instrumental ensemble.

843 Scher 269 ⌐Croesus. Kleine Vöglein, die ihr springet¬ Aria from
        act 2, scene 1. With instrumental ensemble.

844 Lern 78   ⌐Croesus. Seht, wie Herr Elcius¬ Recitative and aria,
        act 2, scene 3. With continuo.

845 Scher 268 ⌐La forza della virtù. Holder Zephyr¬ Aria from act
        2, scene 1. With instrumental ensemble.

846 HAM 267 ⌐Der geliebte Adonis. Fahret wohl¬ Duet from act 2,
        scene 1. With continuo.

847 HAM 148 KERLE, Jacobus de, 1432(ca.)-1591.
        ⌐Exurge, Domine¬ Motet. 4 voices.

        Kettenton, 548.

        King Arthur, 1282.

848 Wolf 64   Kipp- Wipp- und Müntzer-Lied.
        Voice with keyboard. 1623.

849 Scher 304 KIRNBERGER, Johann Philipp, 1721-1783.
        ⌐Polonaise, harpsichord, D major¬

        Kläglicher Abschied, 1410.

850 HAM 84e-f KLEBER, Leonhard, 1495(ca.)-1556.
        ⌐Orgeltabulaturbuch (1524) Selections¬ Preludes in
        mi and re.

851 RR 149   ⌐Orgeltabulaturbuch (1524) Praeambulum¬

        Kleine geistliche Concerte, 1411-1412.

        Kleine Vöglein, 843.

        Kleines Kindelein, 1531.

        Klingende Ton, 1347.

852 Amb 43   KÖLER, David, 1532(ca.)-1565.
        ⌐O du edler Brunn' der Freuden¬ Motet. 4 voices.

        Komm, Gott Schöpfer, heiliger Geist, 1597.

        Komm', heiliger Geist, 218, 1157.

        Kompt, her, ihr Herrn, 1618.

853 Lern 42   KOTTER, Hans, 1480(ca.)-1541.
        ⌐Nach willen dein¬ Chorale prelude.

854 HAM 84g   ⌐Tablature (1513) Organ prelude in F¬

855 Scher 82   ⌐Uss tieffer nodt schry ich zu dir¬ Chorale prelude.

856 Flor 17b   Kränzlein.
        Minnelied. 13th cent.

857 Scher 302 KREBS, Johann Ludwig, 1713-1780.
⌐O Ewigkeit, du Donnerwort⌐ Chorale prelude.

Kreuzigung Christi, 182.

858 HAM 228 KRIEGER, Adam, 1634-1666.
⌐Neue Arien. Adonis Tod⌐ Song, with ritornello.
Voice, strings, and continuo.

859 Flor 135 ⌐Neue Arien. Die Frühlingszeit bringt Lust und Freud⌐
Voice, strings, and continuo. With ritornello.

860 Hamb 58 ⌐Neue Arien. Ihr bleibet nicht Bestand verpflicht⌐
Song. Voice with continuo.

861 Scher 209b ⌐Neue Arien. O schöne Schäferin⌐ Song. 2 voices with
instrumental ensemble.

862 Scher 209a ⌐Neue Arien. Rheinwein muss es sein⌐ Drinking song.
Voice with instrumental ensemble.

863 HAM 249b KRIEGER, Johann, 1651-1735.
⌐Anmuthige Clavier-Übung. Fugue, C major⌐
(HAM mistakenly gives J.P. Krieger's dates.)

864 HAM 249a ⌐Anmuthige Clavier-Übung. Ricercar, F major⌐

865 Scher 235 ⌐Neue musicalische Ergetzlichkeit, Teil 2. No.17⌐
Die Losung ist Geld. Song with bass.

866 Scher 236b KRIEGER, Johann Philipp, 1649-1725.
⌐Flora. Freien ist kein Pferdekauf⌐ Aria from act 2,
scene 6. Bass with continuo.

867 Scher 236a ⌐Procris. Wer's Jagen recht begreifen will⌐ Aria
from act 2, scene 4. Soprano with continuo.

868 RR 167 Ktož jsú boží bojovníci.
Taborite battle song. Czech, 15th cent. 1 voice.

869 Wolf 30 KUGELMANN, Hans, d.1542.
⌐Concentus novi. No.3⌐ Grates nunc omnes. Motet.
3 voices.

870 Scher 109 ⌐Concentus novi. No.31⌐ Nun lob' mein Seel' den
Herren. 5 brass instruments. Text (after Psalm 103)
for tenor part.

Kugelmann, Johann. see KUGELMANN, Hans

871 Flor 148 KUHNAU, Johann, 1660-1722.
⌐Biblische Historien. Il combattimento à David e Goliath. Selections⌐ Sonata for harpsichord from no.1 of
the collection.

872 HAM 261 ⌐Biblische Historien. Der todtkrancke und wieder gesunde Hiskias⌐ Program sonata for harpsichord.

873 Scher 244 ⌐Neuer Clavier-Übung, 1.Teil. Suite, no.6. Gigue⌐

874 Glea 21 Kuninc Rodolp mynnet got.
Lern 16   Minnelied. 13th cent. By "Der Unvürzaghete".
RMA 58

Kunst der Fuge, 115.

Kunt ich schön reines werden Weyb, 1094.

875 Scher 250 KUSSER, Johann Sigismund, 1660-1727.
      ⌐Erindo. Schöne Wiesen, edle Felder⌐ Aria from the
      opera. With continuo.

Kusslied, 742.

Kyrie. see also Cunctipotens

876 Flor 8b Kyrie.
      Gregorian chant. 11th cent.

877 Flor 8a Kyrie.
      Gregorian chant, 11th-13th cent.

Kyrie, 472, 485, 876-883, 1037, 1117.

878 Starr 9 Kyrie, Clemens rector.
      Gregorian chant.

879 Lern 2 Kyrie, Cum jubilo.
      Kyrie IX. Gregorian chant, ca.1100.

880 Hamb 3 Kyrie, Cunctipotens.
      Kyrie IV. Gregorian chant.

881 TEM 15 Kyrie, Cunctipotens.
      Kyrie IV. Organ paraphrase. 14th cent.

Kyrie cunctipotens, 561, 880-881, 928.

882 Starr 12 Kyrie, Fons bonitatis.
      Gregorian chant with trope.

883 OM 42 Kyrie, Rex immense, Pater.
      Trope. 2 voices. Compostela school.

Laetentur coeli et exultet, 744.

Lamentation of Rachel, 1004.

Lamentationes Jeremiae prophetae, 623, 1334, 1614.

Lamento d'Arianna, 1042.

Lamento d'Olimpia, 1043.

Lamento di Tristano, 520.

Lamento sopra la dolorosa perdita..., 574.

Lancan vei la folha, 176.

884 HAM 208 LANDI, Stefano, ca.1590-1655.
      ⌐Il S. Alessio. Act 2. Sinfonia⌐ Overture.
      3 violins, bass instruments, and continuo.

885 HAM 209 ⌐Il S. Alessio. Poca voglia di far bene⌐ Vocal duet
      with instrumental ensemble.

886 OM 77 LANDINI, Francesco, d.1397.
      ⌐L'alma mia piange⌐ Ballata. 3 voices.

887 HAM 53 ⌐Amor c'al tuo suggetto⌐ Ballata. 3 voices.

888 Glea 103 ⌐Angelica biltà⌐ Ballata. 2 voices.
   Scher 23

889	MM 14	⌐Chi più le vuol sapere⌐ Ballata. 2 voices.
890	Lern 29	⌐Chosi pensoso⌐ Canon. 2 voices with instrumental tenor.
891	Glea 106	⌐Una conlonba candid'e gentile⌐ Madrigal. 2 voices.
892	Glea 108	⌐De' dinmi tu che⌐ Madrigal. 3 voices.
893	OM 78	⌐Fa metter bando⌐ Madrigal. 2 voices.
894	Flor 37	⌐Giunta vaga biltà⌐ Ballata. 3 voices.
895	Glea 104 SS 20 Starr 24	⌐Gram piant' agli ochi⌐ Ballata. 3 voices.
896	Wolf 6	⌐El mie dolce sospir⌐ Madrigal. 3 voices.
897	RMA 115	⌐Questa fanciulla⌐ Ballata. 3 voices.
898	Glea 113 HAM 54	⌐Si dolce non sonò⌐ Madrigal. 3 voices.

Landino, Francesco. see LANDINI, F

Langueurs tendres, 98.

899	HAM 71	LANTINS, Arnold de, fl.1431. ⌐Puisque je voy⌐ Rondeau. 3 voices.
900	Scher 41	LANTINS, Hugo de, fl.1415-1430. ⌐A ma damme playsant⌐ Canonic chanson. 3 voices.
901	HAM 72	⌐Ce j'eusse fait⌐ Rondeau. 3 voices.
902	Flor 56 RR 53	LA RUE, Pierre de, d.1518. ⌐L'amour de moy. Confiteor⌐ Excerpt from the isolated Credo. 4 voices.
903	Amb 20	⌐Missa de Sancta Anna. O salutaris hostia⌐ 4 voices. Replaces the first Osanna.
904	Scher 65	⌐Missa de Sancto Anthonio. Kyrie⌐ 4 voices.
905	HAM 92	⌐Missa, L'homme armé. Kyrie I & II⌐ 4 voices.
906	Amb 19	⌐Missa, Tous les regretz. Sanctus⌐ 4 voices.

Lascia al fine de tormentarmi più, 1372.

Lasciatemi morir, 1269.

Lasso che mal accorto, 1333.

907	Scher 126	LASSUS, Orland de, d.1594. ⌐Adoramus te, Christe⌐ Motet. 5 voices. Magnum opus musicum (1604), no.177.
908	HAM 145a	⌐Bon jour, mon coeur⌐ Chanson. 4 voices.
909	Flor 85	⌐Cantate Domino⌐ Motet. 3 voices. From Magnum opus musicum (1604), v.1.
910	Scher 125	⌐Ich armer Mann⌐ Lied. 5 voices.

911 Scher 127   ⌈In hora ultima⌉ Motet. 6 voices. Magnum opus musi-
                    cum (1604), no.414.

912 SS 50   ⌈Libro de villanelle, moresche et altre canzoni. Mato-
                    na, mia cara⌉ Madrigal. 4 voices.

913 HAM 143   ⌈Missa pro defunctis. Introit⌉ 5 voices. From (part
                    2? of) his Patrocinium musices.

914 Nort3 11   ⌈Prophetiae Sibyllarum. Selections⌉ Introduction
                    (Carmina chromatica) and first motet (Virgine matre)
                    4 voices.

915 Starr 47   ⌈Psalmi Davidis poenitentiales. Psalm 6⌉ De profundis.
                    5 voices.

916 HAM 144   ⌈Psalmi Davidis poenitentiales. Psalm 37⌉ Domine, ne
                    in furore tuo. 5 voices.

917 Flor 86   ⌈Qui dort icy?⌉ Chanson. 4 voices.

918 Hamb 75a   ⌈Susanne un jour⌉ Polyphonic chanson. Keyboard set-
                    ting by A. Gabrieli underlaid.

919 Hamb 38   ⌈Tristis est anima mea⌉ Motet. 5 voices. Magnus opus
     MM 23   musicum (1604), no.172.

920 HAM 11   Lauda anima mea Dominum.
     Hamb 2   Psalm 146, with antiphon. Gregorian chant.

                    Lauda Sion, 1173, 1176-1177.

                    Laudate Dominum, 751.

921 MM 1   Laudate pueri.
                        Psalm 113. Gregorian chant.

922 Glea 22   Laude novella sia cantata.
                        Lauda (virelai) 13th cent. 1 voice.

923 MM 1   Laus Deo Patri.
                        Antiphon. Gregorian chant.

                    Lauter dantant, 1134.

                    Lautre jor, 1289.

924 HAM 204   LAWES, Henry, 1596-1662.
                        ⌈Comus. Sweet echo⌉ Aria with continuo, from the
                    masque.

925 Amb 30   LAYOLLE, Francesco de, 1492-ca.1540.
                        ⌈Media vita in morte⌉ Motet. 4 equal voices.

926 Amb 57d   ⌈Questo mostrar si lieto. Part 1⌉ Frottola. 3 voices.
                    Without text.

927 Amb 29   ⌈Salve virgo singularis⌉ Motet. 4 equal voices.

                    Leave off, sad Philomel, 771.

928 Hamb 82   LEBÈGUE, Nicolas Antoine, 1631-1702.
                        ⌈Pièces d'orgues, 2. livre. Kyrie cunctipotens⌉ Pre-
                    lude and fugue.

929 HAM 231   ⌈Pièces d'orgues, 3. livre. Noël, Une vierge pucelle⌉
                    Variations.

LECHNER, Leonhard, d.1606.
　　Deutsche Sprüche von Leben und Tod.　see his ⌐Neue
　　geistliche und welltliche teutsche Gesang⌐

930　Flor 93　　　⌐Historia der Passion und Leidens... Jesu Christi.
　　　　　　　　　1.Teil.　Selections⌐　Chorus, beginning Als nun Jesus
　　　　　　　　　wusste alles.　Texts according to St. John.　4 voices.

931　Hamb 62　　　⌐Neue geistliche und welltliche teutsche Gesang.　Weil
　　　　　　　　　dann so unstet⌐　Motet.　4 voices.　From Deutsche
　　　　　　　　　Sprüche von Leben und Tod.

932　Wolf 42　　　⌐Neue teutsche Lieder (1590)　No.1⌐　Gut Singer und ein
　　　　　　　　　Organist.　Villanella.　3 voices.

933　Scher 294　LECLAIR, Jean Marie, 1697-1764.
　　　　　　　　　⌐Sonata, violin & continuo, op.2, no.4, A major.　Aria⌐
　　　　　　　　　1st movement (rondo).

934　HAM 278　　　⌐Sonata, violin & continuo, op.5, no.12, G major.
　　　　　　　　　Adagio⌐　First movement.

　　　　　　　　Leçons des ténèbres, 377.

935　RMA 43　　　Lectio libri Apocalypsis.
　　　　　　　　　Epistle trope.　Gregorian chant.　Includes a 12th-cent.
　　　　　　　　　French text.

936　HAM 6c　　　Ledovid boruh.
　　　　　　　　　Psalm 144.　Jewish chant.　2 Sephardic and 2 Ashkenazic
　　　　　　　　　versions.　Incomplete.

937　HAM 56　　　LEGRANT, Guillaume, fl.1419.
　　　　　　　　　⌐Credo⌐　2 solo voices and 3-part chorus.

938　Scher 321　LEGRENZI, Giovanni, 1626-1690.
　　　　　　　　　⌐Il Giustino.　Ti lascio l'alma impegno⌐　Aria from
　　　　　　　　　act 1, scene 3.

939　HAM 220　　　⌐Sonatas, op.8.　La buscha⌐　Instrumental ensemble and
　　　　　　　　　continuo.

940　Hamb 88　　　⌐Sonatas, op.8.　La rosetta⌐　Trio-sonata.

941　HAM 126b　LE JEUNE, Claude, d.1600.
　　　　　　　　　⌐Dodecacorde.　Pseaume 35⌐　Deba contre mes debateurs.
　　　　　　　　　5 voices.

942　HAM 138　　　⌐Le printemps.　D'une coline⌐　Chanson.　3-5 voices.

943　Scher 144　　⌐Le printemps.　O rôze reyne des fleurs⌐　Vers mesuré.
　　　　　　　　　4 voices.　No.10 of the collection.

944　Hamb 50　　　⌐Le printemps.　Quiconq' l'amour⌐　Chanson mesurée.
　　　　　　　　　4 voices.　No.25 of the collection.

945　Scher 123　LE MAISTRE, Mattheus, d.1577.
　　　　　　　　　⌐Aus tiefer Not schrei ich zu dir⌐　Chorale.　4 voices.

946　Scher 124　　⌐Bist du der Hensel Schütze⌐　Song.　4 voices.

947　Amb 49a　　　⌐Hör Menschenkind, hör Gottes Wort⌐　Motet.　4 voices.

948   Amb 49b   ⌐Schem dich du tropff⌐ Lied. 4 voices.

949   Lern 22   LEONINUS Magister, fl.1160-1170.
                ⌐Magnus liber organi gradali et antiphonario. Gaude
                Maria⌐ Organum duplum. Notre Dame school.

950   Flor 25   ⌐Magnus liber organi gradali et antiphonario. Haec
                dies⌐ Gradual. Clausula. Incomplete. Notre Dame
                school.

951   TEM 9   ⌐Magnus liber organi gradali et antiphonario. Viderunt
                omnes⌐ Organum duplum. 2 voices. Notre Dame school.

            Leonora, 1013.

952   Scher 225   LEOPOLD I, Emperor of Austria, 1640-1705.
                ⌐Die Erlösung des menschlichen Geschlechts. Jesus
                tot⌐ Aria from the oratorio. With instrumental en-
                semble.

            Leviorum carminum, 1231-1232.

953   HAM 14   Libera me.
                Responsorium. Gregorian chant.

            Lido, o mar, m'aspetta, 1202.

            Liebster Herr Jesu, 235.

            Lisuart und Dariolette, 770.

            Livietta e Tracolo, 1200.

            Livri, 1306.

            Lob des Schnupftabacks, 572.

954   Flor 46a   Lochamer Liederbuch.
      Scher 47   Elend du hast umbfangen mich. Song. 15th cent. Solo
                bass instrument. Text underlaid.

955   HAM 81a   Lochamer Liederbuch.
      Hamb 42a   Mit ganczem Willen. Song. German, 15th cent. 1 voice.

956   HAM 230   LOCKE, Matthew, 1630?-1677.
                ⌐Consort of four parts. Suite no.6. Fantazie⌐ For
                strings. H.136, 6.

            Löwenherz, Richard. see RICHARD I, King of England

957   Scher 15   Lonc le rieu de la fontaine.
                Motet. French, 13th cent. 2 voices. Polytext: Lonc
                le rieu...; Regnat.

            Lonc tans, 1224.

            Lontananza crudel, 1461.

            Look down, O Lord, 249.

958   RR 1   LOQUEVILLE, Richard de, d.1418.
                ⌐Quant compaignons s'en vont juer⌐ Ballade. Voice
                and 2 instruments.

            Lord Salisbury, 640.

959 OM 79   LORENZO da Firenze, 14th cent.
        ⌈Povero çappator⌉ Isorhythmic madrigal. 2 voices.

Losung ist Geld, 865.

Loth to depart, 528.

960 Scher 270   LOTTI, Antonio, d.1740.
        ⌈Alessandro severo. Padre, addio⌉ Da capo aria. With instrumental ensemble.

Luce de questi occhi, 71.

Lucem tuam, 1311.

Ludovicus Pius, 1407.

961 HAM 225   LULLY, Jean Baptiste, 1632-1687.
        ⌈Alceste. Le ciel protège les héros⌉ Recitative and aria from act 1, scene 9.

962 Lern 69   ⌈Alceste. Il faut passer⌉ Opening aria and recitative of act 4.

963 HAM 224   ⌈Alceste. Overture⌉ Strings and continuo.

964 Flor 134   ⌈Armide. Dans un jour de triomphe⌉ Aria from act 1, scene 1. 2 voices with instruments.

965 Scher 234   ⌈Armide. Enfin il est en ma puissance⌉ Recitative from act 2, scene 5.

966 Flor 133   ⌈Armide. Overture⌉ Strings and continuo.
    MM 36

967 Hamb 71   ⌈Cadmus et Hermione. Belle Hermione⌉ Aria, with strings and continuo.

968 Scher 232   ⌈Persée. O mort! venez finir⌉ Aria from act 5, scene 1. With instrumental ensemble.

969 Scher 233   ⌈Roland. Chaconne⌉ Strings and continuo.

970 Hamb 72   ⌈Xerxes. Overture⌉ Instrumental ensemble.

Lust hat mich gezwungen, 34.

Lustgarten neuer teutscher Gesäng, 753-756.

971 Scher 77   LUTHER, Martin, 1483-1546.
        ⌈Deutsche Messe. Sanctus⌉ Chorale tune, Jesaia dem Propheten das geschach. Tenor solo.

972 Wolf 48   LUZZASCHI, Luzzasco, d.1607.
        ⌈Madrigali per cantare e sonare. Cor mio, deh non languire⌉ 2 voices with keyboard.

973 Scher 166   ⌈Madrigali per cantare e sonare. O primavera⌉ Voice with keyboard.

974 SS 51   ⌈Madrigals, 5 voices, book 2. Quivi, sospiri, pianti⌉

Ma bouche rit, 1135.

Ma che temi, 1051.

Ma chiere dame, 697.

Ma fin est mon commencement, 698.

Ma giunge appunto, 747.

Ma maître, 1136.

Ma voix, puissant maître, 1297.

Machaut, Guillaume de. see GUILLAUME de Machaut

975 Ein 25 MACQUE, Giovanni de, 1550(ca.)-1614.
⌈Canzon alla francese, F major⌉ Keyboard or 4 stringed instruments.

976 HAM 174 ⌈Consonanze stravaganti, organ⌉

Madonna mia gentil, 986.

Madonna, per voi ardo, 1557.

Madrigali guerrieri et amorosi, 1044.

977 Wolf 58 MÄRCKER, Matthias.
⌈Galliarda, 4 instruments⌉ 1609.

Maestro, 1026-1030.

Maestro di musica, 1201.

Mag das gesein, 538.

978 OM 94 Magnificat.
Canticle at Vespers. English, ca.1430. 3 voices.

Magnum opus musicum, 907, 909, 911, 919.

979 Scher 107 MAHU, Stephan, 1485(ca.)-1541?
⌈Accessit ad pedes Jesu⌉ Motet. 4 voices.

980 Scher 108 ⌈Ein' feste Burg ist unser Gott⌉ Polyphonic setting (motet) of the chorale. 5 voices.

Mai piu sera lo core, 214.

Maid is like the golden oar, 1195.

Mais nos faz, 44.

Maldito seja quen non loará, 45.

Malheureux cueur, 473.

981 RMA 64 Man mei longe him lives wene.
Song. English, 13th-14th cent. 1 voice.

Manfredina, 521.

982 Flor 17c MANGOLT, Burk, 14th cent.
⌈Fraw, wilt du wissen⌉ Minnelied. Text by Hugo von Montfort.

983 Flor 15a MARCABRU, ca.1100-1150.
⌈Dirai vos senes doptansa⌉ Troubadour song.

984 HAM 18a ⌈Pax in nomine Domini⌉ Troubadour vers. French text.

985 TEM 49 MARCELLO, Benedetto, 1686-1739.
⌈Stravaganze d'amore. Amor tu sei⌉ 2d recitative and aria from the cantata.

Marco Attilio Regolo, 1373.

986	HAM 155	MARENZIO, Luca, 1553-1599. ⌐Madrigals, 5 voices, book 1. Madonna mia gentil¬
987	Ein 18	⌐Madrigals, 5 voices, book 2. Io piango et ella il volto¬
988	MM 27 Nort 3	⌐Madrigals, 5 voices, book 6. S'io parto, io moro¬
989	Scher 165	⌐Madrigals, 5 voices, book 9. Solo e pensoso¬
990	Hamb 55 Scher 140	⌐Villanelle, 3 voices, book 1. In un boschetto¬
991	Flor 104	⌐Villanelle, 3 voices, book 3. Io son ferito¬

Margarite, fleur de valeur, 190.

992	Flor 38 RMA 61 Scher 25	Maria, muoter reinû maît. Geisslerlied, 14th cent. 1 voice.
993	RR 34	Maria zart. German melody, with text. Includes excerpt from an Obrecht setting.

Maria zart, 993, 1400.

994	Scher 19	Mariae assumptio. Motet. 13th cent. 2 voices with 3 instruments. Polytext: Mariae assumptio; Huius chori.

Mariam gubernans, 316.

995	Scher 182	MARINI, Biagio, 1597-1665. ⌐Affetti musicali, op.1. Sonata, La gardana¬ Violin and continuo.
996	Flor 125	⌐Affetti musicali, op.1. Sonata, La ponte¬ Violin or cornet and continuo.
997	HAM 199	⌐Arie, madrigali et correnti, op.3. Romanesca, violin & continuo¬ Variations.
998	Scher 183	⌐Sonate, symphonie, canzoni... op.8. Sonata, A minor¬ Sonata per il violino per sonar con due corde. Violin and continuo.

Mars, Bellone, 1300.

Martinella, 810.

Más quiero morir, 501.

Más vale trocar, 502.

999	HAM 175	MASCHERA, Fiorenzo, 1540(ca.)-1584. ⌐Canzoni da sonare a 4 voci, libro 1º. No.14¬ 4 instruments.

Maschera, Florentio. see MASCHERA, Fiorenzo

Mass... see also Missa...; Messa...

Mass for Easter Sunday, 298-300.

67

1000 Scher 2a Mass, In festis duplicibus I. Gloria and Sanctus.
    Gregorian chant.

1001 Flor 9 Mass, In festis duplicibus I. Kyrie.
    Gregorian chant. 10th cent. With trope.

1002 OM 62 Mass of Barcelona. Agnus Dei.
    French, mid-14th cent. 4 voices.

1003 OM 90 Mass, Salve sancta parens. Agnus Dei.
    English, ca.1435. 4 voices.

1004 RMA 46 Massacre of the innocents (Liturgical drama) Lamentation
    of Rachel.

Matona, mia cara, 912.

1005 Scher 24 MATTEO da Perugia, fl.1402-1416.
    ⌐Pour bel acueil⌐ Chanson balladée (rondeau) 3 voices.

1006 OM 81 ⌐Serà quel zorno⌐ Ballata. 3 voices.

Matthäuspassion, 118-120.

1007 Scher 267 MATTHESON, Johann, 1681-1764.
    ⌐Die heylsame Geburth und Menschwerdung unsers Herrn...
    Fürchtet euch nicht⌐ Aria from the Christmas oratorio.
    With instrumental ensemble.

1008 Lern 49 MAUDUIT, Jacques, 1557-1627.
    ⌐Chansons mesurées de Ian-Antoine de Baïf. Vous me
    tuez⌐ 4 voices.

Maus d'amer, 15.

May, 1089, 1630.

May no rash intruder, 735.

Mayenzeit, 1090.

Mazza, 1327.

1009 Scher 197 MAZZOCCHI, Domenico, 1592-1665.
    ⌐Dialoghi e sonetti. Nisus erat portae custos. Planc-
    tus matris Euryali⌐ Recitative. Voice and continuo.

Media vita, 660, 925, 1108.

Megdlein sind von Flandern, 67.

Mein freundlich's B., 1131, 1436.

Mein G'müth ist mir verwirret, 754.

Mein vleis und mus ich nie hab gspart, 1437.

Mein's traurens ist, 776.

Melopoiae sive harmoniae, 1523.

Mente tota, 536.

Menuet de Poitou, 385.

Mercè grido piangendo, 629.

Merope, 1500.

1010   Scher 32a   Merthe of alle this londe.
                  Christmas carol. English, ca.1420. 3 voices.

1011   HAM 210   MERULA, Tarquinio, d.ca.1665.
                  ⌐Canzoni, libro 2. Canzon detta la Vesconta⌐ Trio-
                  sonata.

1012   Scher 184   ⌐Canzoni overo sonate concertate. La Strada⌐
                  3 strings and continuo.

1013   Wolf 43   MERULO, Claudio, da Correggio, 1533-1604.
                  ⌐Canzoni d'intavolatura d'organo, libro 1. La Leonora⌐

1014   Ein 22   ⌐Ricercari d'intavolatura d'organo, libro 1. F major⌐

1015   TEM 29   ⌐Toccate d'intavolatura d'organo, libro 1. Secondo
                  tono⌐ Toccata 5.

1016   HAM 153   ⌐Toccate d'intavolatura d'organo, libro 2. F major⌐

1017   Scher 149   ⌐Toccate d'intavolatura d'organo, libro 2. Quinto tono⌐

1018   Flor 89   ⌐Toccate d'intavolatura d'organo, libro 2. Settimo
                  tono⌐

1019   Hamb 80   ⌐Toccate d'intavolatura d'organo, libro 2. Ottavo tono⌐

               Mes esperis se combat, 699.

               Meskin es hu, 1130.

1020   Scher III   MESOMEDES, 1st cent.
                  ⌐Aeide musa moi phile⌐ Hymn to the muse. Song.

1021   HAM 7b   ⌐Chionoblepharou pater⌐ Hymn to the sun. Song.
       Scher IV

1022   Flor 2b   ⌐Nemesi pteroessa biu ropa⌐ Hymn to Nemesis. Song.
       Scher V

               Messa di Santa Cecilia, 1374.

               Messe de Nostre Dame, 700-702.

               Messiah, 724-729.

               Mia region è questa, 608.

1023   Scher 74   MICHA, D   15th-16th cent.
                  ⌐Integer vitae⌐ 4 voices, or voice and lute. Petrucci,
                  Frottole I (1504), 44.

1024   Amb 54   MICHAEL, Rogier, ca.1554-1619.
                  ⌐Ein' feste Burg ist unser Gott⌐ Chorale. 4 voices.

               Micrologus, 681.

               Mie dolce sospir, 896.

1025   Wolf 16   Mijn morken gaf mij een jonck wijf.
                  Song. Flemish, 15th cent. 3 voices.

               MILÁN, Luis, ca.1500-1562.
               Libro de música de vihuela de mano. see his ⌐El maes-
               tro⌐

1026 Hamb 53   ⌈El maestro. Durandarte⌉ Romanze. Voice with vihuela.
      Scher 96a

1027 HAM 97b   ⌈El maestro. Durandarte⌉ Villancico. 4 voices.

1028 Scher 96b   ⌈El maestro. Falai miña amor⌉ Villancico. Voice with
                  vihuela.

1029 HAM 121   ⌈El maestro. Fantasia, B-flat major⌉ Vihuela.

1030 HAM 97a   ⌈El maestro. O dulce y triste memoria⌉ Villancico.
                  4 voices.

              Milano, Francesco da. see FRANCESCO da Milano

              Millan. see MILÁN, Luis

              Mille ducas, 1474.

1031 Glea 31   Mira lege, miro modo.
                     Organum, conductus style. Strophic hymn. Early 12th
                     cent. 2 voices. St. Martial school.

              Miserere mei, Deus, 88.

              Misero che farò, 1546.

              Miserunt ergo sortem, 296.

              Missa... see also Mass...; Messa...

              Missa apostolorum, 315.

              Missa caput, 475.

              Missa cujusvis toni, 1137.

1032 HAM 15a   Missa Cunctipotens (Mass IV) Kyrie.
                     Gregorian chant.

1033 Scher 92   Missa Cunctipotens, organ. Sanctus.
                     (Attaingnant, 1531) Includes the liturgical chant.

              Missa de Beata Virgine, 316, 539.

              Missa de Sancta Anna, 903.

              Missa de Sancto Anthonio, 904.

              Missa di San Carlo, 584.

              Missa duarum facierum, 1070.

              Missa festivale, 221.

1034 Starr 1   Missa in dominica resurrectionis.
                     Gregorian chant. (Officium majoris hebdomadae, Liber
                     usualis).

              Missa la sol fa re mi, 425.

              Missa mi-mi, 1140, 1154.

              Missa Papae Marcelli, 1178-1180.

              Missa paschalis, 812.

              Missa pro defunctis, 913.

              Missa prolationum, 1141-1142.

Missa sine nomine, 1122, 1273.

Missa super Dringhs, 222.

Missa super epitaphium Mauritii, 1363.

1035 TEM 13 Missa tornacensis. Agnus Dei.
The Tournai mass. French, 14th cent. 3 voices.

1036 OM 61 Missa tornacensis. Kyrie.
The Tournai mass. French, 14th cent. 3 voices.

Missa tubae, 386.

Mit ganczem Willen, 955, 1190.

Mitilde, mio tesor, 1375.

1037 Scher 18 Mois de mai.
Motet. Goliard song, 13th cent. 3 voices. Polytext:
El mois de mai; De se debent; Kyrie.

Mois de Mai, 1037, 1287.

Mon chier amy, 480.

Mon Dieu me paist sous sa, 665.

1038 Glea 13 MONIOT d'Arras, ca.1190-1240.
RMA 55 ⌐Ce fut en mai⌐ Trouvère sequence.
Starr 13

1039 HAM 295 MONN, Matthias Georg, 1717-1750.
⌐Symphony, D major. Allegro⌐ Last movement.

Monsiers almaine, 63, 158.

1040 HAM 146b MONTE, Philippe de, 1521-1603.
⌐Missa, Cara la vita. Sanctus⌐ 5 voices.

1041 Scher 178 MONTEVERDI, Claudio, 1567-1643.
⌐L'incoronazione di Poppea. Pur ti miro⌐ Final duet.
With continuo.

1042 Scher 177 ⌐Lamento d'Arianna⌐ Aria, with continuo.

1043 Flor 113 ⌐Lamento d'Olimpia. Voglio morir⌐ Recitative. Voice
and continuo.

1044 HAM 189 ⌐Madrigali guerrieri et amorosi. Combattimento di Tancredi e Clorinda. Non schivar, non parar⌐ Aria.
Voice with instrumental ensemble.

1045 Flor 116 ⌐Madrigals, book 1. Se nel partir da voi⌐ 5 voices.

1046 HAM 188 ⌐Madrigals, book 4. Ohimè, se tanto amate⌐ 5 voices.

1047 Starr 69 ⌐Madrigals, book 5. Cruda Amarilli⌐ Madrigal.
5 voices.

1048 Nort3 15 ⌐Madrigals, book 9. Zefiro torna⌐ Ciaccona. 2 voices
and continuo.

1049 Hamb 69 ⌐L'Orfeo. Act 4. Selections⌐ 5-part chorus (Pietade
oggi), aria (Qual honor), recitatives, and instrumental
interludes.

1050	Nort3 14	⌐L'Orfeo. Coro di ninfe e pastori⌐ 5-part chorus with instrumental ensemble.
1051	HAM 187	⌐L'Orfeo. Ma che temi⌐ Recitative from act 4. Solo voices and continuo.
1052	Lern 63 SS 37 Starr 72	⌐L'Orfeo. Possente spirto⌐ Aria from act 3. With instrumental ensemble. Includes written-out parts and embellishments as in the original score.
1053	Scher 176	⌐L'Orfeo. Rosa del cie⌐ Aria, with continuo.
1054	MM 31 Nort 4 Nort3 14	⌐L'Orfeo. Tu sei morta⌐ Recitative. Tenor and continuo.
1055	Flor 114	⌐Il ritorno d'Ulisse in patria. Ulisse troppo errò⌐ Aria di Giunone, with continuo.
1056	Wolf 53	⌐Scherzi musicali (1607) La violetta⌐ 3 voices with instrumental ensemble.
1057	Flor 115	⌐Selva morale e spirituale. Gloria. Domine Deus rex celestis⌐ Motet. 3 voices.
1058	SS 44	⌐Vespro della Beata Vergine. Domine ad adjuvandum⌐ 6 voices and instrumental ensemble.

Montezuma, 671.

1059	HAM 128	MORALES, Cristóbal, 1500(ca.)-1553. ⌐Emendemus in melius⌐ Motet. 5 voices.
1060	TEM 23	⌐Magnificat, octavi toni⌐ 4-6 voices. From Magnificats (1545).
1061	Amb 62	⌐Sancte Antoni pater monachorum⌐ Motet. 4 voices.
1062	HAM 159	MORLEY, Thomas, 1557-1603? ⌐Balletts. My bonny lass⌐ 5 voices.
1063	Flor 103	⌐Canzonets, 3 voices. See, mine own sweet jewell⌐
1064	Nort3 12	⌐Madrigals, 5 voices. Sing we and chant it⌐
1065	Starr 41	⌐Pavane and galliard, harpsichord, F major⌐ From the Fitzwilliam virginal book.

Moro lasso, 631.

1066	Lern 23	Mors. Organum quadruplum, based on Alleluia resurgens. Notre Dame school.

Mors, 1066-1067.

1067	Lern 23	Mors a primi. Motet, ca.1200. Formed by the addition of texts to a Notre Dame organum quadruplum on Mors. Polytext: Mors a primi; Mors, que stimuo; Mors morsu; Mors.

Mors e vita, 833.

Mors morsu, 1067.

Mors, que stimuo, 1067.

1068	OM 13	Mors vite porpitia.

      Conductus, ca.1200. Notre Dame school.

Morte di S. Giuseppe, 1202.

1069 Lern 35   MORTON, Robert, d.1475.
        ⌈N'araige jamais mieulx⌉ Rondeau. 3 voices.

      MOULU, Pierre, d.mid-16th cent.
        Missa, Alma redemptoris. see his ⌈Missa duarum facie-rum⌉

1070 RR 55   ⌈Missa duarum facierum. Kyrie I⌉ 4 voices. Versions with and without observance of some rests. Also known as Missa, Alma redemptoris.

Mourisque, 1472.

Mourn for they servant, 196.

1071 Glea 65 Mout me fu grief.
      SS 1c   Motet. Late 13th cent. 3 voices. Polytext: Mout me fu grief; Robin m'aime; Portare.

1072 Min 27   MOUTON, Jean, d.1522.
        ⌈In illo tempore Maria Magdalene⌉ Motet. 4 voices.

1073 Min 59   ⌈La rouse du moys de may⌉ Chanson. 6 voices.

1074 Scher 66   ⌈Salve mater salvatoris⌉ Mirror canon. 4 voices.

1075 HAM 240 MUFFAT, Georg, 1653-1704.
        ⌈Apparatus musico-organisticus. Passacaglia⌉ Abridged.

1076 Scher 251   ⌈Florilegium, no.1. Selections⌉ Gavotte and minuet in A minor. 4 strings and keyboard.

1077 Flor 139   ⌈Florilegium, no.2. Indissolubilis amicitia. Selec-tions⌉ Suite, string orchestra: Sarabande pour le genie de l'amitié, and Menuet.

1078 HAM 280 MUFFAT, Gottlieb, 1690-1770.
        ⌈Componimenti musicali, harpsichord. Suite, no.1. Final⌉

1079 Scher 292   ⌈Componimenti musicali, harpsichord. Suite, no.1. Ouverture⌉

Munday, John. see MUNDY, John

1080 OM 54   Mundus vergens.
        Conductus. French, ca.1210. 4 voices.

1081 HAM 177 MUNDY, John, d.1630.
        ⌈Goe from my window, harpsichord. Selections⌉ Varia-tions. Lacks variations 3 and 6. Fitzwilliam virginal book, v.1, 153.

Musae Sioniae, 1262-1265.

1082 Min 5   MUSET, Colin, 13th cent.
        ⌈Quand je voi yver retorner⌉ Trouvère ballade.

Musica boscareccia, 1395.

1083   Glea 24   Musica enchiriadis ⌈9th-cent. codex⌉ Selections.
      HAM 25b   Examples of parallel organum. (see also 1404)
      Hamb 12
      MM 6
      OM 37
      Starr 15

                Musicalische Blumen-Büschlein, 545.

1084   Scher 287   Musicalische Rüstkammer (1719)
                Menuet, and aria. Voice and harp.

                Musicalische Tafelfreudt, 1254.

                Musicalischer Bergkreyen, 554.

                Musicalischer Studentenmuht, 1618.

                Musikalisches Allerley, 98.

                Musikalisches Opfer, 121.

                Musikalisches Vielerley, 99.

                My bonny lass, 1062.

                My heart is inditing, 1283.

                My heart was so free, 1196.

1085   HAM 103   My Lady Carey's dompe.
                Variations on a ground. English, ca.1525. Harpsichord.

                My Ladye Nevells book, 244.

                My love is all madness, 1195, 1198.

                My thoughts are winged, 452-453.

                Myn vroud ist gar czugangyn, 559.

                Mystery sonatas. see BIBER, HIF ⌈Sonatas...⌉

                N'araige jamais mieulx, 1069.

                Nach willen dein, 777, 853.

                Nachdem David war redlich, 1348.

1086   HAM 152   NANINI, Giovanni Maria, 1545(ca.)-1607.
                ⌈Hic est beatissimus⌉ Motet. 3 voices. Soprano and
                bass in strict canon.

                Narrabimus omnes, 292.

1087   HAM 122   NARVAEZ, Luis de, 16th cent.
                ⌈El Delphin de música. O gloriosa Domina⌉ Variations.
                Lute.

                Nas mentes senpre tẽer, 46.

                Nasce l'aspro, 72.

                Nativitas gloriose Virginis Marie, 1213.

1088   Wolf 4   Nato nobis hodie.
                Hymn, 14th cent. 2 voices.

Natus ante saecula, 1109.

1089	HAM 20c	NEIDHART von Reuenthal, 13th cent. ⌐Der May⌐ Minnelied.

1090	Glea 21	⌐Mayenzeit⌐ Minnelied.
1091	OM 32	⌐Owê dirre sumerzît⌐ Minnelied (bar).
1092	MM 5	⌐Willekommen mayenschein⌐ Minnelied.
1093	HAM 20d	⌐Winder wie ist⌐ Minnelied (bar).

Nel mezzo a sei paon, 645.

Nemesi pteroessa biu ropa, 1022.

Nenciozza mia, 824.

Neue Bauernschwanz, 649.

Neue musicalische Ergetzlichkeit, 865.

1094	Hamb 85	NEUSIEDLER, Hans, 1508 or 9-1563. ⌐Kunt ich schön reines werden Weyb, lute⌐
1095	HAM 105b	⌐Ein new künstlich Lautten Buch. Der Juden Tantz⌐
1096	Flor 72	⌐Ein newes Lautenbüchlein. Der Nunnen tantz⌐
1097	Wolf 29	⌐Ein newgeordent künstlich Lautenbuch. Gassenhawer⌐
1098	Scher 93	⌐Ein newgeordent künstlich Lautenbuch. Praeamble, no.3⌐

New ground, 1284.

Newes christliches Lied, 1599.

Newsidler, Hans. see NEUSIEDLER, Hans

Next winter comes slowly, 1278.

1099	Wolf 7	NICCOLÒ da Perugia, 14th cent. ⌐Dappoi che'l sole⌐ Caccia. 3 voices.
1100	Wolf 7	⌐Passando con pensier per un boschetto⌐ Caccia. 3 voices.

Nightingale so pleasant, 251.

Nisus erat portae custos, 1009.

Nò, il pomo nò, 327.

1101	Glea 47 HAM 25c Hamb 15	Nobilis, humilis. Hymn to St. Magnus. Organum (gymel) ca.1200. 2 voices.
1102	Scher 137	NÖRMIGER, August, 1560(ca.)-1613. ⌐Dances, keyboard. Selections⌐ Der heiligen drei Könige Aufzug; Polnischer Tanz; Teutscher Tanz.
1103	Ein 17	NOLA, Giovanni Domenico da, 1510(ca.)-1592. ⌐Canzoni villanesche, libro 2. Tri ciechi siamo povri inamorati⌐ 3 voices.

Non abbandona mai Iddio, 748.

Non al suo amante, 819.

Non è tempo d'aspettare, 205, 287.

Non orphanum, 1287.

1104   Scher 89a   Non podrio anar plus mau.
         Provençal song, ca.1525. 1 voice.

Non schivar, non parar, 1044.

Non val aqua, 1526.

Non vos relinquam, 59, 248.

1105   Min 8   Nota.
         Dance. 2 instruments.

Notenbuch der Anna Magdalena Bach, 122.

Notes pour moi, 79.

1106   HAM 16a   NOTKER Balbulus, 840-912.
         ⌐Christus hunc diem¬ Sequence to the Gregorian chant
         alleluia Dominus in Sina. Chant included.

1107   Scher 4   ⌐Haec est sancta solemnitas¬ Gregorian sequence.

1108   Scher IX   ⌐Media vita in morte sumus¬ Antiphon. Gregorian
         chant.

1109   Scher X   ⌐Natus ante saecula¬ Gregorian sequence, in nativi-
         tate Domini.

1110   Ein 5   ⌐Psallat ecclesia¬ Gregorian sequence.

1111   Scher XI   ⌐Stirpe Maria¬ Gregorian sequence, in nativitate S.
         Mariae.

Notre Dame school. see Part 2: Subjects

Nous sommes de l'ordre de St. Babouin, 352.

1112   Glea 43   Novus miles sequitur.
       Hamb 21   Conductus. Vers. Hymn on the death of Thomas à Becket,
         1170. Early 13th cent. 2 voices.

Now I needs must part, 454.

1113   OM 103   Now wolde y fayne.
         Song. English, mid-15th cent. 2 voices.

1114   Lern 32   Nowel syng we.
         Carol. English, 15th cent. 2 voices.

Nu al'erst, 1602.

1115   Glea 23   Nû ist diu.
         Geisslerlied (lai segment) 13th cent. 1 voice.

Nun komm, der Heiden Heiland, 123, 238, 1364.

Nun lasst uns Gott, 1161.

Nun lob' mein Seel' den Herren, 870.

Nunc dimittis, 598.

Nunnen tantz, 1096.

Nuove musiche, 262-268.

Nus hom, 344.

O allmächtiger Gott, 219.

O beate Basili, 1123.

O begl'anni dell'oro, 375.

O dolce vita mia, 1619.

O Domine Jesu Christe, 430, 1566.

O du armer Judas, 220.

O du edler Brunn' der Freuden, 852.

O du Liebe meiner Liebe, 1336.

O dulce y triste memoria, 1030.

O dulcissima Maria, 1563.

O Elslein, 1438.

O Ewigkeit, du Donnerwort, 124, 857.

O gloriosa Domina, 1087.

O Haupt voll Blut und Wunden, 118.

O Herr, hilf, 1424.

1116 OM 50   O homo considera.
                   Isorhythmic motet. English, early 14th cent. 4 voices.
                   Polytext: O homo considera; O homo de pulvere; Filiae
                   Jerusalem; textless contratenor.

O homo de pulvere, 1116.

O Lord, increase my faith, 639.

O Lord, my God, 784.

O magnum mysterium, 594, 1569-1571, 1620.

O mia cieca e dura sorte, 285, 288.

1117 Nort3 2   O miranda dei karitas.
                   Motet. 13th cent. 3 voices. Polytext: O miranda;
                   Salve mater salutifera; Kyrie.

O mort, venez finir, 968.

O nostre Dieu, 664.

O pierulin dov' estu? 1547.

O primavera, 1973.

1118 Glea 7   O roma nobilis.
      Starr 13   Goliard song. 11th cent. 1 voice.

O rosa bella, 486, 650.

O rôze reyne des fleurs, 943.

O salutaris hostia, 903, 1621.

O schöne Schäferin, 861.

O schönes Weib, 540.

O tu cara scienzia mia, 646.

O vos omnes, 1124, 1572.

1119	OM 82	O virgo splendens. Caça. Spanish, 14th cent. 3 voices.
1120	Amb 7	OBRECHT, Jacob, d.1505. ⌐Ave regina¬ Motet. 4 voices.
1121	Amb 8	⌐Forseulement¬ Chanson. 4 voices.
1122	HAM 77	⌐Missa sine nomine. Selections¬ Kyrie I (4 voices) and Agnus II (2 voices).
1123	HAM 76a	⌐O beate Basili. Part 1¬ Motet. 4 voices.
1124	HAM 76b Scher 54	⌐O vos omnes¬ Motet. 3 voices.
1125	Flor 48 Hamb 33 MM 18	⌐Parce, Domine¬ Motet. 3 voices.
1126	Amb 12	⌐Salve regina¬ 3 equal voices. Includes the original chants.
1127	Amb 11	⌐Se bien fait¬ Chanson. 4 voices.
1128	Amb 10	⌐La tortorella¬ 4 voices.
1129	HAM 78	⌐Tsaat een meskin¬ Instrumental canzona. 4 parts.
1130	Amb 9	Weltliches Lied ohne Text (probably Meskin es hu) 4 voices. The first motif was used by several compo- sers for various texts.

Occhi, perchè piangete, 1462.

Occhi tuoi, 345.

Ochi mei lassi, 289.

1131	Flor 64	OCHSENKUN, Sebastian, 1521-1574. ⌐Die Weyber mit den Flöhen, lute¬ Transcription of Senfl's Mein freundlich's B. (see 1436).
1132	Amb 6	OCKEGHEM, Jean de, d.1497. ⌐Fugue in epidiatesseron, 3 instruments¬ Based on his Lauter dantant?
1133	Amb 2	⌐Je nay deul¬ Chanson. 4 voices.
1134	Amb 3	⌐Lauter dantant¬ Chanson. 3 voices.
1135	HAM 75 Wolf 14	⌐Ma bouche rit¬ Virelai. 3 voices.
1136	HAM 74	⌐Ma maîtresse¬ Virelai. 3 voices.
1137	Amb 1	⌐Missa cujusvis toni. Selections¬ Sanctus, 4 voices; Benedictus, 2-3 voices.
1138	HAM 73	⌐Missa, L'homme armé. Selections¬ Kyrie and Agnus III. 4 voices.
1139	Starr 28	⌐Missa, L'homme armé. Kyrie¬ 4 voices.

1140 Lern 36   ⌐Missa mi-mi. Agnus Dei⌐ 4 voices.

1141 RR 31   ⌐Missa prolationum. Kyrie 1⌐ 4 voices.

1142 MM 17   ⌐Missa prolationum. Sanctus. 1st section⌐ 4 voices.

1143 Flor 47   ⌐Missa, Le serviteur. Osanna⌐ 4 voices.

1144 Amb 4   ⌐Se ne pas jeulx⌐ Chanson. 3 voices.

1145 Amb 5   ⌐Se vostre ceur⌐ Chanson. 3 voices.

1146 Scher 52   ⌐Ut heremita solus⌐ Motet. 4 instruments.

1147 Glea 46   ODINGTON, Walter, fl.ca.1325.
                  ⌐Ave mater Domini⌐ Rondellus. 3 voices.

             Of all the birds that I do know, 152.

1148 TEM 8   Ogne homo.
                  Lauda. 13th-14th cent. 1 voice.

             Ogni indugio d'un amante, 731.

             Oh ponder well, 1195.

             Ohimè, se tanto amate, 1046.

             Oho, so geb' der Mann einen Pfennig, 1439.

             Oimè, che vegg'io? 603.

             Oimè il cor, 206, 290.

             Olimpia, 1376.

             Omnipotens genitor, 1535.

1149 Glea 63   On parole de batre.
     HAM 33b   Motet. 13th cent. 3 voices. Polytext: On parole...;
                  A Paris; Frèse nouvele.

             Opera nova de balli, 165.

1150 MM 4   Or la truix.
                  Trouvère virelai. 12th-13th cent.

             Or sus, serviteurs, 207, 669.

             Orfeo, 1049-1054, 1339.

1151 HAM 17a   Orientis partibus.
                  Song of the ass (Conductus ad tabulam) From the
                  12th-cent. liturgical drama at Beauvais.

             Orlando generoso, 1463.

             Ormindo, 309-310.

             Orphenica lyra, 580.

1152 Flor 59   Orsù car' Signori.
     HAM 96   Canto carnascialesco, "per scriptores". Italian,
     Wolf 18   ca.1500. 4 voices.

1153 Amb 27   ORTO, Marbriano de, d.1529.
                  ⌐Ave Maria gratia plena⌐ Motet. 4 voices.

1154 Amb 28   ⌐Missa mi-mi. Agnus Dei⌐ 4 voices.

1155	Flor 67	OSIANDER, Lucas, 1534-1604.
		⌐Christ lag in Todesbanden⌐ Chorale. 4 voices.
1156	Hamb 61a	⌐Gott sei gelobet und gebenedeiet⌐ Chorale. 4 voices.
1157	Scher 143	⌐Komm, heiliger Geist⌐ Chorale. 4 voices.

Oswald von Wolkenstein. see WOLKENSTEIN, Oswald von

Où courez vous? 1298.

Oublier veul, 29.

Owê dirre sumerzît, 1091.

Oy comamos y bebamos, 503.

1158	Scher 243	PACHELBEL, Johann, 1653-1706.
		⌐Ach Herr, mich armen Sunder⌐ Chorale prelude.
1159	Hamb 92a	⌐Gelobet seiest du, Jesu Christ⌐ Chorale prelude.
1160	HAM 251	⌐Magnificat, keyboard instrument, F major⌐ Fugue.
1161	Ein 35	⌐Nun lasst uns Gott, dem Herren⌐ Chorale prelude.
1162	HAM 250	⌐Suite, harpsichord, A-flat major⌐ Suite "ex gis".
1163	Lern 83	⌐Suite, harpsichord, E major⌐
1164	MM 37	⌐Toccata, organ, E minor⌐
1165	HAM 190c	⌐Vater unser im Himmelreich⌐ Chorale prelude.
1166	Flor 141	⌐Vom Himmel hoch, da komm ich her⌐ Chorale prelude.
1167	Min 103	PADOVANO, Annibale, ca.1527-1575.
		⌐Aria della battaglia⌐ 8 wind instruments.

Padre, addio, 960.

1168	RR 162	PAIX, Jakob, 1556-ca.1624.
		⌐Ungarescha, organ⌐ Dance.

Palästinalied, 1602.

1169	Scher 122	PALESTRINA, Giovanni Pierluigi da, 1525?-1594.
		⌐Adjuro vos⌐ Motet. 5 voices.
1170	HAM 142	⌐Alla riva del Tebro⌐ Madrigal. 4 voices.
1171	Flor 83	⌐De lamentatione Hieremiae⌐ Motet. 4 voices.
1172	Lern 50	⌐Exsultate Deo⌐ Psalm 80. Motet. 5 voices.
1173	Starr 52	⌐Lauda Sion⌐ Motet. 4 voices.
1174	SS 3b	⌐Missa, Aeterna Christi munera. Gloria⌐ 4 voices.
1175	Nort3 10	⌐Missa, Ascendo ad patrem. Sanctus⌐ 5 voices.
1176	Starr 54	⌐Missa, Lauda Sion⌐ 3-5 voices.
1177	Scher 121	⌐Missa, Lauda Sion. Benedictus⌐ 3 voices.
1178	HAM 140	⌐Missa Papae Marcelli. Agnus Dei I⌐ 6 voices.
1179	Hamb 39	⌐Missa Papae Marcelli. Agnus Dei II⌐ 7 voices.
1180	Nort 2	⌐Missa Papae Marcelli. Kyrie⌐ 6 voices.

1181	MM 24	⌐Missa, Veni sponsa Christi. Agnus Dei I⌐ 4 voices.
1182	Flor 84	⌐Quando dal terzo cielo⌐ Madrigal. 6 voices.
1183	HAM 141	⌐Sicut cervus⌐ Motet. 4 voices.
1184	Scher 224	PALLAVICINO, Carlo, 1630-1688. ⌐Diocletiano. Sinfonia⌐ Overture. Instrumental ensemble.
1185	Flor 50a SS 4b Starr 30	Pange lingua. Gregorian hymn. Words by St. Thomas Aquinas, 1263.

Pange lingua, 392, 426-429, 481, 1185, 1511.

1186	OM 51	Pange melos lacrimosum. Conductus with cauda. French, ca.1200. 2 voices.

Panis quem ego dabo, 346, 764.

Par maintes foys, 1543.

Parce, Domine, 1125.

Parthenia, 226.

Paseábase el rey, 581.

1187	TEM 35	Passamezzo d'Italie. 4 instruments. 16th cent.

Passando con pensier per un boschetto, 1100.

Pater noster, 1622.

Patience, 156.

Patrocinium musices, 913.

1188	OM 104	PAUMANN, Conrad, 1410(ca.)-1473. ⌐Fundamentum organisandi. Selections⌐ Preambulum super fa, and Enavois.
1189	Flor 46b Scher 48	⌐Fundamentum organisandi. Elend du hast umbfangen mich⌐ 2-part organ setting.
1190	HAM 81b Hamb 42b	⌐Fundamentum organisandi. Mit ganczem Willen⌐
1191	HAM 104	Pavane. French, ca.1530. Harpsichord.

Pavane d'Angleterre, 626.

1192	Scher 91	Pavane et galliarde. Keyboard. (Attaingnant, 1530).

Pax in nomine Domini, 984.

Pazienza di Socrate, 457.

Pazzia senile, 148.

1193	OM 17	PEIROL, ca.1160-1225. ⌐Del sieu tort farai esmenda⌐ Troubadour vers.

Pellicana, 319.

1194 OM 65   PENNARD, 14th cent., supposed composer.
⌐Gloria⌐ Isorhythmic mass movement. English, ca.1390.
4 voices.

1195 Scher 281 PEPUSCH, John Christopher, 1667-1752.
⌐The beggar's opera. Selections⌐ 3 arias: A maid is
like the golden oar, and Oh ponder well, from act 1;
My love is all madness, from act 3, scene 1.

1196 Flor 151 ⌐The beggar's opera. Act 1. Selections⌐ Arias from
scene 13: Pretty Polly say, and My heart was so free.
With continuo.

1197 HAM 264b ⌐The beggar's opera. Hither, dear husband⌐ Aria from
act 3, scene 12.

1198 HAM 264a ⌐The beggar's opera. My love is all madness⌐ Aria
     Scher 281 from act 3, scene 1.

Per quel vago boschetto, 261, 1207, 1211.

1199 Lern 39 Perchè ciascun difender de l'onore.
Florentine carnival song, late 15th cent. 4 voices.

Perfidissimo volto, 267.

1200 TEM 50 PERGOLESI, Giovanni Battista, 1710-1736.
⌐Livietta e Tracollo. Ecco il povero Tracollo⌐ Recitative and aria from act 1.

1201 HAM 286 ⌐Il maestro di musica. Le virtuose⌐ Aria with instrumental ensemble.

1202 Flor 169 ⌐La morte di S. Giuseppe. Il lido, o mar, m'aspetta⌐
Recitative and aria with continuo.

1203 HAM 287 ⌐La serva padrona. Lo conosco⌐ Duet with instrumental
ensemble.

1204 Ein 36 ⌐La serva padrona. Stizzoso mio stizzoso⌐ Aria.

1205 Scher 275 ⌐Stabat mater. Eja mater, fons amoris⌐ Aria. Alto
with instrumental ensemble.

1206 Flor 170 ⌐Trio-sonata, C major. Allegro⌐

1207 Scher 171 PERI, Jacopo, 1561-1633.
⌐Euridice. Selections⌐ Prolog: Io che d'alti sospir.
Per quel vago boschetto. Cruda morte. Solo voices
and chorus, with continuo.

1208 Flor 98b ⌐Euridice. Ben nochier costante⌐ Terzetto e coro.
With continuo.

1209 HAM 182 ⌐Euridice. Funeste piaggi⌐ Recitative with continuo.

1210 Flor 98a ⌐Euridice. Gioite al canto mio⌐ Aria. Tenor with continuo.

1211 Flor 99a ⌐Euridice. Per quel vago boschetto⌐ Voice and continuo. Incomplete.
(For the complete aria, see 1207.)

1212 Hamb 68 ⌐Euridice. Sia pur lodato il ciel⌐ Recitative, with
3 flutes and continuo.

1213	MM 9	PEROTINUS Magister, fl.1180-1236. ⌐Alleluia, Nativitas gloriose Virginis Marie┐ Organum. 3 voices. Notre Dame school.
1214	Glea 7 HAM 17c	⌐Beata viscera┐ Conductus. 1 voice. Notre Dame school.
1215	Flor 26	⌐Haec dies┐ Gradual. Clausula. Incomplete. Notre Dame School.
1216	Lern 24	⌐Salvatoris hodie┐ Conductus. 3 voices. Notre Dame school.
1217	HAM 17d	⌐Sol oritur in sydere┐ Conductus. Notre Dame school.
1218	Glea 36	⌐Viderunt. Vide prophecie┐ Organum quadruplum. Notre Dame school.
1219	HAM 19c	PERRIN d'Agincourt, 13th cent. ⌐Douce dame debonnaire┐ Trouvère ballade.
1220	HAM 19d	⌐E ma dame┐ Trouvère rondeau.
1221	OM 23	⌐Il covient qu'en la chandoile┐ Trouvère chanson cap- caud, vers form.
1222	Glea 11 HAM 19b	⌐Quant voi en la fin┐ Trouvère ballade. Voice with chorus.

Persée, 968.

Perugia, Matteo da. see MATTEO da Perugia

1223	Ein 13	PESENTI, Michele, ca.1475-1525. ⌐Dimmi un poco che vuol dire┐ Frottola. Voice and 3 instruments.

Petite Camusette, 431.

1224	HAM 34	PETRUS de Cruce, d.ca.1300. ⌐Aucun ont trouvé┐ Motet. 3 voices. Polytext: Aucun; Lonc tans; Annuntiantes.
1225	Wolf 34	PETSCHIN, Gregor. ⌐Dort niden an dem Rheyne, lute┐ Lautenlied, 1558. Text given separately.
1226	Ein 26	PEUERL, Paul, 1575(ca.)-1625? ⌐Neue Padouan, Intrada, Däntz und Galliarde. Suite, C major┐ Variations suite, for organ or instruments.
1227	Flor 112	⌐Neue Padouan, Intrada, Däntz und Galliarde. Suite, D major┐ 4 instruments.
1228	Hamb 79 Scher 157	⌐Neue Padouan, Intrada, Däntz und Galliarde. Suite, F major┐ 4 instruments.
1229	Scher 221	PEZEL, Johann, 1639-1694. ⌐Hora decima. Turmsonate┐ In one movement. 5 brasses.
1230	Hamb 91	⌐Intrada, 5 brasses, B-flat major┐ From Intraden... 1685.

Pfoben Swancz, 151.

1231 Wolf 39-40 PHALÈSE, Pierre, ca.1510-1573.
        ⌜Leviorum carminum, book 1. Selections⌝ Allemande
        'S medelÿn and Bransle d'ecosse. 4 instruments.

1232 Scher 134 ⌜Leviorum carminum, book 1. Pavane and galliarde
        ferrarese⌝ 4 instruments.

1233 OM 58 PHILIPPE de Vitry, 1291-1361.
        ⌜Vos qui admiramini⌝ Isorhythmic motet. 4 voices.
        Polytext: Vos qui admiramini; Gratissima virginis;
        Gaude gloriosa; textless contratenor.

1234 Scher 174 PHILIPS, Peter, 1561-1628.
        ⌜Amarilli mia bella, virginals⌝

1235 HAM 145b ⌜Bon jour, mon coeur, keyboard⌝ Incomplete.

1236 RMA 11 Photizon, photizon.
        Ode from the Kanon for the morning of Easter Sunday.
        Byzantine chant. Echos I.

        Piangerò, 722.

1237 HAM 154b PICCHI, Giovanni, fl.1621.
        ⌜Intavolatura di balli d'arpicordo. Passamezzo⌝ Vari-
        ations. Sections 1, 2, 4 only.

1238 Ein 31 PICCINNI, Niccolò, 1728-1800.
        ⌜La buona figliuola. Overture⌝ Italian overture.
        Keyboard score. Alternate title of opera: La cecchina
        nubile.

        La cecchina nubile. see his ⌜La buona figliuola⌝

1239 HAM 300 ⌜Le faux Lord. Achetez à ma boutique⌝ Aria.

        Pierce, Edward. see PIERS, Edward

1240 Flor 36 PIERO, Maestro, 14th cent.
        ⌜Con dolce brama⌝ Caccia. 3 voices.

        Pieros li Borgnes. see TRESORIERS de Lille

        Pierre de la Croix. see PETRUS de Cruce

1241 Min 95 PIERS, Edward, fl.ca.1600.
        ⌜Hey, Trola, there boys there⌝ Hunting song. 4 voices.
        Includes facsimile of 16th-cent. hunting calls.

        Pietade oggi, 1049.

1242 Scher I PINDAR, 518-436 BC.
        ⌜Chrysea phorminx⌝ Song. Melodie zur ersten pythi-
        schen Ode. Unison voices.

1243 HAM 284 PLATTI, Giovanni, 1690-1763.
        ⌜Sonata, harpsichord, op.1, no.2, C major. Allegro⌝
        Last movement.

1244 Flor 166 ⌜Sonata, harpsichord, op.4, no.5, C minor. Allegro⌝
        third movement.

        Planctus matris Euryali, 1009.

        Play of the three kings, 796.

Plorate filii, 295.

Plus dure que un dyamant, 703.

Poca voglia di far bene, 885.

1245	TEM 40	POGLIETTI, Alessandro, d.1683. ⌐Capriccio über das Henner und Hennengeschrey, harpsi- chord⌐ 2d part of the 3d harpsichord suite.
1246	HAM 236	⌐Rossignolo. Aria allemagna. Selections⌐ 6 of the 23 variations in the harpsichord suite.

Poiche ad Irene, 600.

Pois preyatz me, senhor, 177-178.

1247	Flor 88	Polish dance. German, ca.1580. Harpsichord. With proportio.
1248	RR 173	Polish dance, lute.
1249	RMA 9	Pollà ta 'étē tōn Basiléōn. Byzantine chant, 15th cent. Acclamation to Emperor John VI Palaiologos.
1250	OM 30	Polorum regina. Pilgrim song (ballo rodð) Spanish, 14th cent.

Pomo d'oro, 324-328.

Pomone, 274-275.

1251	RMA 12	Pomosch moîa ot Gospoda. Russian Znamenny chant, 17th cent. Psalm 122, 2.

Ponte, 996.

1252	TEM 2	Populе meus. Improperia of the Mass for Good Friday. Gallican chant.

Por conforter ma pesance, 1507.

1253	Wolf 44	Por la puente Juana. Villancico. Spanish, 16th cent. 3 voices.

Portare, 1071.

1254	Wolf 60	POSCH, Isaac, d.1623? ⌐Musicalische Tafelfreudt. Paduane 6⌐ 5 instruments.

Possente spirto, 1052.

Pour bel acueil, 1005.

Pour ce se d'amer me dueil, 1508.

Pour mon cuer, 687.

Pour ung plaisir, 387, 588.

Pourtant si je suis brunette, 1445.

Povero çappator, 959.

1255	Scher 37	POWER, Lionel, d.1445. ⌐Anima mea, 3 voices⌐ Motet.

1256 OM 67   ⌐Beata progenies⌐ Motet. 3 voices. Contains elements
     RMA 125   of conductus and English discant.

1257 OM 66   ⌐Credo⌐ Isolated mass movement. 3 voices.

1258 Wolf 9   ⌐Gloriosae virginis Mariae⌐ Motet. 3 voices.
                    (For a version with added 4th voice, see his Works,
                      edited C. Hamm, v.1, no.12.)

1259 Hamb 29   ⌐Missa, Alma redemptoris mater. Selections⌐ Sanctus
                 and Agnus Dei I. 3 voices. Includes the antiphon
                 chant.

1260 HAM 63   ⌐Sanctus⌐ Isolated mass movement. 4 voices. Original
                 chant underlaid.

1261 OM 53   Praemii dilatio.
                 Conductus with caudae. French, ca.1210. 3 voices.

1262 Scher 161 PRAETORIUS, Michael, 1571-1621.
                 ⌐Musae Sioniae, book 6. Geborn ist der Emanuel⌐
                 Christmas carol. Solo voices and 4-part chorus.

1263 Scher 162   ⌐Musae Sioniae, book 6. Ich dank dir, lieber Herre⌐
                 Motet. 4 voices.

1264 HAM 167a   ⌐Musae Sioniae, book 9. Vater unser im Himmelreich⌐
                 Chorale. 2 voices.

1265 Flor 117   ⌐Musae Sioniae, book 9. Vom Himmel hoch⌐ Motet.
                 3 voices.

1266 HAM 167b   ⌐Terpsichore. Ballet du Roy pour sonner après⌐ Suite.
                 4 instruments.

1267 Wolf 59   ⌐Terpsichore. Bransle simple de Novelle⌐ 5 instru-
                 ments.

                Preis des Schöpfers, 97.

                Prendés i garde, 688.

                Pretty Polly say, 1196.

                Prety ducke there was, 153.

                Preussische Festlieder, 495.

                Primavera, 1581-1582.

                Printemps, 942-944.

1268 MM 22   Prinzen-Tanz. Proportz.
                 Lute. ca.1550.

                Procris, 867.

                Prophetiae Sibyllarum, 914.

1269 HAM 222   PROVENZALE, Francesco, 1627-1704.
                 ⌐Il schiavo di sua moglie. Lasciatemi morir⌐ Aria
                 from act 1, scene 8. With strings and continuo.

                Psallat, 60.

1270 OM 47   Psallat chorus.
                    Franconian motet. ca.1250. 3 voices. Polytext: Psal-
                    lat chorus; Eximie pater; Aptatur. From Franco of
                    Cologne's Ars cantus mensurabilis.

                 Psallat ecclesia, 1110.

                 Psalmen Davids, 1416-1417.

                 Psalmi Davidici, 589.

                 Psalmi Davidis poenitentiales, 915-916.

                 Psaumes de David, 664-669, 1478.

1271 HAM 28h   Pucelete bele.
                    Motet. ca.1250. 3 voices. Polytext: Pucelete bele;
                    Je languis; Domino. Notre Dame school. Includes the
                    clausula, ca.1200, from which the motet is derived.

                 Puer natus est nobis, 804.

                 Pues que jamás, 504.

                 Puis que la douce, 692.

                 Puisque je voy, 899.

                 Puisque m'amour, 232, 487.

1272 Scher 179 PUJOL, Juan, 1573-1626.
                    ⌈Requiem. Introit⌉ 4 voices.

1273 OM 91   PULLOIS, Johannes, d.1478.
                    ⌈Missa sine nomine. Gloria⌉ 3 voices.

                 Pur ti miro, 1041.

1274 Lern 72   PURCELL, Henry, 1659-1695.
                    ⌈Dido and Aeneas, Z.626. Ah Belinda⌉ Aria from act 1.

1275 Lern 71   ⌈Dido and Aeneas, Z.626. Overture⌉ Strings and con-
                    tinuo.

1276 HAM 255   ⌈Dido and Aeneas, Z.626. When I am laid in earth⌉
      Hamb 74   Aria from act 3, with preceding recitative (Thy hand,
      Nort 7   Belinda).
      Nort3 19
      Starr 102

1277 Starr 102   ⌈Dido and Aeneas, Z.626. With drooping wings⌉ Final
                    chorus of act 3.

1278 Flor 144   ⌈The fairy queen, Z.629. Next winter comes slowly⌉
                    Aria from act 4. With instrumental ensemble.

1279 HAM 256   ⌈Fantasias, 3-7 viols. Z.735⌉ Fantasia for 4 viols in
                    G minor.

1280 Scher 248a   ⌈I gave her cakes, Z.256⌉ Catch. 3 voices.

1281 Hamb 95   ⌈I will love Thee, O Lord, Z.67⌉ Anthem. 4-part cho-
                    rus and bass recitative, with continuo.

1282 Scher 247   ⌈King Arthur, Z.628. I call you all⌉ Aria and chorus
                    from act 1.

1283	Scher 246	⌈My heart is inditing, Z.30. Alleluja⌉ Final chorus from the anthem. 8 voices and strings.
1284	Flor 145 MM 38	⌈A new ground, harpsichord, Z.682, E minor⌉ Chaconne. From the second part of Musick's hand-maid.
1285	SS 10	⌈Suite, harpsichord, Z.660, G major⌉ No.1.

Put me not to rebuke, 390.

1286	OM 96	PYAMOUR, John, fl.1420-1430. ⌈Quam pulchra es⌉ Marian antiphon. Motet. 3 voices.

Quae nutritos, 530.

Qual honor, 1049.

Quam pulchra es, 488, 1286.

Quand je voi yver retorner, 1082.

Quand je vous ayme ardentement, 83.

Quand me souvient, 388.

Quando dal terzo cielo, 1182.

Quando ritrova, 534.

Quant compaignons s'en vont juer, 958.

1287	OM 45	Quant florist. Motet. French, ca.1225. 3 voices. 2 versions shown in a single score. Polytext: Quant florist; Non orphanum <u>or</u> El mois de Mai; Et gaudebit.

Quant je le voi, 529.

1288	Ein 7	Quant li rossignols s'escrie. Troubadour song.
1289	HAM 28i	Quant revient. Motet. ca.1250. 3 voices. Polytext: Quant revient; Lautre jor; Flos filius. Notre Dame school. With related clausula and Latin motet.
1290	HAM 32b	Quant voi. Motet. 13th cent. 3 voices. Polytext: Quant voi; Virgo virginum; Hec dies. Includes the Latin text (O mitissima) replaced by the French.

Quant voi en la fin, 1222.

Quant voi la rose, 499.

Quelle audace, 281.

Quem terra, pontus, 225.

Quen Jesucrist' essa Madre, 47.

Questa fanciulla, 897.

Questo mostrar si lieto, 926.

Qui au conseil, 208.

1291 OM 9   Qui confidunt in Domino.
                 Tract at Mass on the 4th Sunday of Lent. Gregorian
                 chant.

                 Qui dat nivem, 384.

                 Qui dort icy? 917.

                 Qui es promesses, 704.

                 Qui secuntur, 531.

1292 Scher 2b   Qui sedes.
                 Gradualvers nach der römischen und der Mailänder Liter-
                 gie. Gregorian and Ambrosian chant.

                 Quia fecit mihi magna, 1587.

                 Quia vidisti me Thoma, 750.

                 Quiconq' l'amour, 944.

                 Quinte estampie real, 522.

                 Quis dabit oculis nostris, 1440.

                 Quis est homo, 271.

1293 Scher 16   Quis tibi Christe meritas.
                 Conductus. 13th cent. Voice and 2 instruments.
                 Notre Dame school.

                 Quivi, sospiri, pianti, 974.

1294 Ein 6   Radit aetas aurea.
                 Conductus. English, 12th cent. 2 voices.

1295 Flor 15b   RAIMBAUT de Vaqueiras, 1155-1207.
      Glea 13   ⌐Kalenda maya⌐ Estampie. Troubadour song.
      HAM 18d
      Hamb 6
      Scher 11

                 Ramage des oiseaux, 1307.

                 Rambaut. see RAIMBAUT

1296 Scher 296 RAMEAU, Jean Philippe, 1683-1764.
                     ⌐Castor et Pollux. Gavotte⌐ Instrumental ensemble.

1297 Scher 297a   ⌐Castor et Pollux. Ma voix, puissant maître⌐ Recita-
                 tive, act 1, scene 4. With continuo.

1298 Flor 159   ⌐Castor et Pollux. Où courez vous?⌐ Recitative and
                 aria from act 1, scene 2. 2 voices and continuo.

1299 MM 41   ⌐Castor et Pollux. Séjour de l'éternelle paix⌐ Aria
                 and recitative.

1300 Scher 297b   ⌐Dardanus. Mars, Bellone⌐ 4-part chorus, act 1, scene
                 3. With instrumental ensemble.

1301 HAM 277   ⌐Dardanus. Sommeil⌐ "Rondeau tendre", for strings and
                 continuo, accompanying a dream scene.

1302 Scher 296   ⌐Les Indes galantes. Musette en rondeau⌐ Instrumental
                 ensemble.

1303 Flor 160   ⌈Pièces de clavecin. Les soupirs⌉

1304 Scher 296   ⌈Pièces de clavecin. Tambourin⌉

1305 Starr 115   ⌈Pièces de clavecin. Les tourbillons⌉

1306 SS 55a   ⌈Pièces de clavecin en concert. Selections⌉ La livri
                    (trio-sonata) and La forqueray (fugue) 2 strings and
                    harpsichord.

1307 HAM 276   ⌈Le temple de la gloire. Ramage des oiseaux⌉ Final
                    scene from the opera-ballet. Solo voice with instrumen-
                    tal ensemble.

                    Rappresentazione di anima e di corpo, 303-306.

                    Rare, 329.

1308 Glea 1   Ratelthes en tois.
                       Byzantine chant. Hirmologion.

                    Ratto delle Sabine, 25.

                    Ravenscroft, Giovanni. see RAVENSCROFT, John

1309 Ein 29   RAVENSCROFT, John, d.1708.
                       ⌈Trio-sonata, violins & continuo, op.1, no.2, B minor⌉
                    Church sonata. Keyboard score. Formerly attributed to
                    Antonio Caldara.

                    Recordata est Jerusalem, 377.

1310 TEM 1   Redde mihi.
                       Psalmellus for Quadragesima. Ambrosian chant.

1311 HAM 120b   REDFORD, John, d.1547.
                       ⌈Lucem tuam, organ⌉

1312 HAM 120a   ⌈Veni redemptor gentium, organ⌉

                    Regina coeli, 223.

1313 Scher 139a   REGNART, Jacob, 1540(ca.)-1599.
                       ⌈Tricinia. Venus, du und dein Kind⌉ Villanella.
                    3 voices. P.292.

1314 Scher 139b   ⌈Tricinia. Wer sehen will zween lebendige Brunnen⌉
                    Villanella. 3 voices. P.299.

                    Regnat, 957.

                    Regola Rubertina, 609.

1315 Scher 252   REICHE, Johann Gottfried, 1667-1734.
                       ⌈Neue quatricinia, cornet & 3 trombones. No.15⌉ In C
                    minor; originally in D minor.

                    Reimbautz. see RAIMBAUT

                    Reine des coeurs, 383.

1316 Scher 207   REINKEN, Jan Adamsz, 1623-1722.
                       ⌈Schweiget mir vom Weibernehmen, harpsichord⌉ Partita
                    (variations)

                    Reis florios, 715.

Reniement de saint-Pierre, 336.

1317 Glea 2 Requiem aeternam.
      Mozarabic chant. Antiphon from the Office of the dead.

1318 Hamb 61b RESINARIUS, Balthasar, 1485(ca.)-1544.
      ⌈Gott sei gelobet und gebenedeiet⌉ Chorale-motet.
      4 voices.

      Resta di darmi noia, 632.

      Resurgens, 61, 1066.

1319 Scher 216 REUSNER, Esaias, 1636-1679.
      ⌈Delitiae testudinis. Selections⌉ Courante, sarabande
      and gigue. Lute.

1320 HAM 233 ⌈Delitiae testudinis. Suite, D minor. Praeludium⌉
      Lute.

      Rex immense, Pater, 883.

1321 OM 40   Rex omnia tenens.
      Troped Benedicamus Domino. Organum. St. Martial
      school.

1322 RMA 40 Rex sanctorum.
      Procession hymn. Gregorian chant.

1323 HAM 37 Rex virginum.
      Trope. 13th cent. 2 voices.

      Rheinwein muss es sein, 862.

      Rhétorique des dieux, 618-621.

1324 Glea 8   RICHARD I, King of England, 1157-1199.
    HAM 19a ⌈Ja nus hons pris⌉ Trouvère rotrouenge.
    Hamb 7

1325 Glea 8   RICHART de Semilli, 13th cent.
      ⌈Autr'ier tout seus⌉ Trouvère rotrouenge. Voice with
      chorus.

1326 OM 16   RIGAUT de Berbezilh, ca.1170-1210.
      ⌈Atressi com l'olifanz⌉ Troubadour canso.

1327 Wolf 56 ROGNONI, Giovanni Domenico.
      ⌈La mazza⌉ Canzona. 4 instruments. From his Canzoni,
      1605.

      Rinaldo, 730-732.

      Ritorno d'Ulisse in patria, 1055.

      Robin m'aime, 14, 1071.

      Rodelinda, 733.

1328 Glea 15 Roi a fait.
      Trouvère song. 12th cent.

      Roland, 969.

1329 Flor 29 Roma gaudens jubila.
    HAM 38   Conductus. 13th cent. 2 voices. Notre Dame school.
    RMA 89

Roman de Fauvel. see Fauvel

Romanesca, 997.

1330 OM 1   ROMANOS, fl.500.
       ⌐He parthenos semeron⌐ Kontakion. Byzantine chant.

1331 Hamb 48b   RORE, Cipriano de, 1516-1565.
       ⌐Madrigals, book 5. Da le belle contrade⌐ 5 voices.

1332 Scher 106   ⌐Musica sopra le stanze del Petrarca in laude della
       Madonna. No.3⌐ Vergine pura. Madrigal. 5 voices.

1333 Hamb 48b   ⌐Musica sopra le stanze del Petrarca in laude della
       Madonna. No.15⌐ Lasso che mal accorto. Madrigal.
       5 voices.

Rosa das rosas, 48.

Rosa del cie, 1053.

Rosaura, 1377-1378.

1334 HAM 218   ROSENMÜLLER, Johann, 1619(ca.)-1684.
       ⌐Lamentationes Jeremiae. Aleph: Ego vir⌐ Voice and
       continuo.

1335 Scher 220   ⌐Sonate da camera, strings & continuo (1670) Suite,
       C minor. Sinfonia⌐ Overture.

1336 Scher 290   ROSENROTH, Knorr von, supposed composer.
       ⌐O du Liebe meiner Liebe⌐ Sacred song. 1684. Voice
       with keyboard.

Rosetta, 940.

Rosignuolo, 1379.

1337 Wolf 50   ROSSETER, Philip, 1568-1623.
       ⌐Airs, 1601. When Laura smiles⌐ Song. Voice with
       lute and bass viol.

1338 HAM 203   ROSSI, Luigi, 1598-1653.
       ⌐Io lo vedo. Io lo vedo⌐ Da capo aria from the cham-
       ber cantata. Voice and continuo.

1339 Scher 199   ⌐L'Orfeo. Dormite, begl'occhi⌐ Slumber song.
       3 female voices with continuo.

Rossignol en amour, 381.

Rossignolo, 1246.

1340 Scher 141   ROSTHIUS, Nicolaus, 1542(ca.)-1622.
       ⌐Ich stieg auf einen Birnenbaum⌐ Lied. 4 voices.

Rouse du moys de may, 1073.

1341 HAM 291   ROUSSEAU, Jean Jacques, 1712-1778.
       ⌐Le devin du village. Allons danser⌐ Aria.

Royne du ciel, 353.

Rügen, Wizlaw von. see WIZLAW von Rügen

1342 RMA 59   RUMELANT, Meyster, 13th cent.
       ⌐Daz Gedeones wollenvlius⌐ Minnelied.

1343 HAM 302 RUTINI, Giovanni Maria, 1723-1797.
⌐Sonata, harpsichord, op.6, no.6, E-flat major. Allegro⌐ Last movement.

1344 Flor 176 ⌐Sonata, violin & harpsichord, op.14, no. , B-flat major. Rondo⌐

S'amours tous amans, 705.

S'il estoit nulz, 705.

S'io parto, io moro, 988.

1345 TEM 22 SACHS, Hans, 1494-1576.
⌐Gesangweise⌐ Meisterlied. Text based on Psalm 94.

1346 HAM 24   ⌐Der gülden Ton⌐ Meisterlied (bar).
      Hamb 10

1347 Flor 65   ⌐Der klingende Ton⌐ Meisterlied.
      RR 146

1348 Lern 21   ⌐Nachdem David war redlich⌐ Meisterlied.

1349 Scher 78 ⌐Silberweise⌐ Meisterlied.

1350 Ein 8   ⌐Wacht auff ir werden christen⌐ Meisterlied.

Sacrae symphoniae, 596-599.

Saint Martial school. see Part 2: Subjects

1351 OM 102   Saint Thomas honour we.
Carol. English, ca.1430. 3 voices.

Sainte Marie virgine, 657.

Sainte Nicholaes, godes druth, 658.

Saltarello. see also Estampie

1352 HAM 59b Saltarello.
Estampie. Italian, 14th cent. 1 instrument.
(Not the same as 1353 or 1354)

1353 Flor 40 Saltarello.
14th cent. (see also 1352)

1354 Lern 26 Saltarello.
      OM 87   Italian, 14th cent. 1 instrument.
      SS 7   (see also 1352)
      Scher 28

Salutatio prima, 1441.

Salvator mundi, 1483.

Salvatoris hodie, 1216.

Salve mater salutifera, 1117.

Salve mater salvatoris, 1074.

Salve regina, 680, 778, 782, 1126, 1401, 1567.

Salve sancta parens, 1003.

1355 Wolf 3   Salve virgo.
        Motet. 13th cent. 3 voices. Polytext: Salve virgo;
        Verbum caro; Veritatem.

        Salve virgo singularis, 927.

1356 Flor 167   SAMMARTINI, Giovanni Battista, 1701-1775.
        ⌐Sonate notturne, 2 violins & continuo, op.7. No.4.
        Allegro⌐ 2d movement. Trio-sonata.

1357 HAM 283   ⌐Symphony, string orchestra, D major. Allegro⌐
        First movement.

        Sancta Maria non est, 489.

        Sancte Antoni pater monachorum, 1061.

        Sancti Jacobi, 478.

1358 SS 5a   Sanctus.
        Gregorian chant, 11th-12th cent. From Mass Ordinary
        VIII.

1359 OM 64   Sanctus.
        Mass movement in English descant style, ca.1370.
        3 voices.

        Sanctus, 490, 1260, 1358-1359.

        Sanguis Jesu, 197.

        Sans cuer, 706.

        Sans roch, 157.

        Sant'Alessio, 884-885.

1360 HAM 21c   Santo Lorenzo.
        Modified ballata. Lauda, 13th cent.

        Saprei morir, 583.

1361 Scher 223   SARTORIO, Antonio, 1620(ca.)-1681.
        ⌐Adelaide. Act. 1. Selections⌐ Sinfonia, and aria
        Vittrici schieri.

        Saul, was verfolgst du mich, 1425.

1362 Amb 53   SCANDELLO, Antonio, 1517-1580.
        ⌐Bonzorno madonna⌐ Canzone napolitana (villanella)
        4 voices.

1363 Amb 50   ⌐Missa super epitaphium Mauritii. Selections⌐ 6 sec-
        tions. 3-7 voices.

1364 Amb 51   ⌐Nu komm der Heiden Heiland⌐ Motet. 5 voices.

1365 Scher 132   ⌐Vorria che tu cantass'⌐ Canzona napolitana (villa-
        nella) 4 voices.

1366 Amb 52   ⌐Der wein, der schmeckt mir also wol⌐ Drinking song.
        6 voices.

        Scaramella, 432.

1367 TEM 44   SCARLATTI, Alessandro, 1660-1725.
                    ⌐La caduta de' Decemviri. Overture⌐ Strings and con-
                    tinuo.

1368 HAM 260   ⌐Concerto grosso, no.3, F major. Selections⌐
                    First 3 of 5 movements. Strings and continuo.

1369 Scher 259   ⌐Griselda. Figlio, dove t'ascondo⌐ Recitative from
                    act 2, scene 4. 2 soloists with continuo.

1370 HAM 259   ⌐Griselda. Sinfonia⌐ Overture to the opera.

1371 Scher 258   ⌐Gl'inganni felici. Tisbe, si può haver pietà⌐
                    Buffo scene. Duet. With continuo.

1372 Scher 260   ⌐Lascia al fine de tormentarmi più⌐ Solo cantata.
                    With continuo.

1373 Scher 90   ⌐Marco Attilio Regolo. Sinfonia⌐ Overture. 7 instru-
                    ments and continuo.

1374 Lern 74   ⌐Messa di Santa Cecilia. Sanctus⌐ Mass no.2, A major.
                    5 solo voices, 5-part chorus, strings, and continuo.

1375 HAM 258   ⌐Mitilde, mio tesor⌐ Chamber cantata. Solo voice and
                    continuo.

1376 Hamb 73   ⌐Olimpia. Sinfonia⌐ Overture to the chamber cantata.
                    Strings and continuo.

1377 Flor 147   ⌐La Rosaura. Sinfonia⌐ Overture to the opera.

1378 Flor 146   ⌐La Rosaura. Son si dolci le catene⌐ Aria from act 1,
                    scene 2. With instrumental ensemble.

1379 Lern 73   ⌐Il rosignuolo⌐ Solo cantata. Voice with continuo.

1380 MM 42   SCARLATTI, Domenico, 1685-1757.
      Nort3 27   ⌐Sonata, harpsichord, K.11, C minor⌐

1381 HAM 274   ⌐Sonata, harpsichord, K.175, A minor⌐

1382 Starr 93   ⌐Sonata, harpsichord, K.456, A major⌐

1383 Scher 282   ⌐Sonata, harpsichord, K.519, F minor⌐

1384 Flor 158   ⌐Sonata, harpsichord, K.534, D major⌐

1385 Scher 282   ⌐Sonata, harpsichord, K.544, B-flat major⌐

1386 HAM 195a   SCHEIDEMANN, Heinrich, 1596(ca.)-1663.
                    ⌐Prelude, organ, D minor⌐

1387 HAM 195b   ⌐Prelude and fugue, organ, D minor⌐

1388 Flor 124   SCHEIDT, Samuel, 1587-1654.
                    ⌐Tabulatura nova. Da Jesus an dem Kreuze stund. Selec-
                    tions⌐ Variations. Organ.

1389 Lern 66   ⌐Tabulatura nova. Gelobet seist du, Jesu Christ⌐
                    Variations. Organ.

1390 HAM 190a   ⌐Tabulatura nova. Vater unser im Himmelreich⌐ Chorale
                    prelude.

1391 Scher 185   ⌐Tabulatura nova. Warum betrübst du dich, mein Herz⌐
                    Variations. Organ.

1392 HAM 196   ⌐Tabulatura nova. Wehe, Windgen, wehe⌐ Variations.
                   Organ.

1393 Flor 123   SCHEIN, Johann Hermann, 1586-1630.
                       ⌐Banchetto musicale. No.14. Padouana⌐ 5 strings.

1394 Lern 67   ⌐Banchetto musicale. No.15⌐ Suite in G major.
                   5 instruments.

1395 Scher 187a   ⌐Musica boscareccia II. Viel schöner Blümelein⌐
                   3 voices.

1396 Scher 188   ⌐Opella nova. Th.1. Gelobet seist du, Jesu Christ⌐
                   Choralkonzert. 3 voices with continuo.

1397 TEM 38   ⌐Opella nova. Th.2. Erschienen ist der herrliche
                   Tag⌐ Cantata. With continuo.

1398 Scher 187b   ⌐Venus Kräntzlein. Gleichwie ein kleines Vögelein⌐
                   5 voices.

                   Schem dich du tropff, 948.

1399 Scher 245   SCHENK, Johann, 1656?-ca.1712.
                       ⌐Scherzi musicali, op.6. No.11. Fugue⌐ From a sonata
                   for viola da gamba and continuo.

                   Schernito, 612.

                   Scherzi musicali, 1056, 1399.

                   Schiavo di sua moglie, 1269.

1400 HAM 101   SCHLICK, Arnolt, b.ca.1460.
                       ⌐Tabulaturen etlicher Lobgesang. Maria zart⌐ Organ.

1401 HAM 100   ⌐Tabulaturen etlicher Lobgesang. Salve regina⌐ Organ.
      Hamb 43

1402 Scher 111   SCHMELTZL, Wolfgang, ca.1500-1561.
                       ⌐Der Felber sprach⌐ Quodlibet. 4 voices. Polytext:
                   Der Felber sprach; Ich sach einsmals; Von edler art;
                   Ich hab mich redlich ghalten.

1403 Scher 136   SCHMID, Bernhard, 1535-1592.
                       ⌐Galliarde des Admirals auss Frankreich⌐ Keyboard.

                   Schmücke dich, o liebe Seele, 391.

                   Schöne Wiesen, edle Felder, 875.

1404 HAM 25a   Scholia enchiriadis ⌐9th-cent. treatise⌐ Selections.
                   Examples of parallel organum. (see also 1083)

1405 Scher 289   SCHOLZE, Johann Sigismund, 1705-1750.
                       ⌐Die singende Muse an der Pleisse, 1.Teil. Selections⌐
                   Menuet and Murky. Songs with keyboard.

1406 Amb 55   SCHRÖTER, Leonhart, fl.1580.
                       ⌐Te Deum laudamus. German⌐ 2 4-part choruses.

1407 Scher 293   SCHÜRMANN, Georg Caspar, 1672(ca.)-1751.
                       ⌐Ludovicus Pius. Wohnt noch Mitlied⌐ Da capo aria
                   from the opera. With strings.

1408   Hamb 65   SCHÜTZ, Heinrich, 1585-1672.
⌐Geistliche Chormusik. Selig sind die Toten⌐ Motet.
6 voices. B.391.

1409   Hamb 96   ⌐Historia von der Auferstehung Jesu Christi. Selec-
tions⌐ Nos.6-7: Recitative and duet (Sie haben den
Herren) With strings and continuo. B.50.

1410   Wolf 65   ⌐Kläglicher Abschied⌐ Voice and continuo. B.52.

1411   Flor 122   ⌐Kleine geistliche Concerte. Wann unsre Augen schlafen
ein⌐ Cantata. 2 voices and continuo. B.316.

1412   Scher 190   ⌐Kleine geistliche Concerte. Was hast du verwirket⌐
Cantata. Solo voice with organ. B.307.

1413   Flor 121   ⌐Passion (St. Luke) Selections⌐ Nos.1 and 20-33 (Introitus and Chapter 22/33-38) Chorus and recitatives.
B.480.

1414   Hamb 66   ⌐Passion (St. Matthew) Selections⌐ Nos.10-25: Recitatives and chorus. B.479.

1415   Scher 192   ⌐Passion (St. Matthew) Selections⌐ Nos.12(in part)-29,
124(in part)-130. Recitatives and chorus. B.479.

1416   Scher 189   ⌐Psalmen Davids (1628) Es ist fürwahr ein kostlich
Ding⌐ Psalm 92. 4 voices. B.190a.

1417   Scher 189   ⌐Psalmen Davids (1628) Ich heb' mein' Augen sehnlich
auf⌐ Psalm 121. 4 voices. B.226a.

1418   Scher 191   ⌐Die sieben Worte Christi am Kreuz. Selections⌐
Nos.2-9: Sinfonia and recitatives. B.478.

1419   HAM 201b   ⌐Die sieben Worte Christi am Kreuz. Selections⌐
Nos.18-21: recitatives with chorus. B.478.

1420   HAM 201a   ⌐Die sieben Worte Christi am Kreuz. Da Jesus an dem
Kreuze stund⌐ No.1 (Introitus) Chorus. 5 voices.
B.478.

1421   Starr 95   ⌐Symphoniae sacrae. Pt.1, no.10⌐ Veni de libano.
2 voices with instrumental ensemble. B.266.

1422   Lern 64   ⌐Symphoniae sacrae. Pt.1, no.13⌐ Fili mi, Absalon.
Cantata. Bass voice, 4 trombones, and continuo. B.269.

1423   Ein 27   ⌐Symphoniae sacrae. Pt.2, no.5⌐ Der Herr ist meine
Stärke. Motet. Voice, 2 violins, and continuo. B.345.

1424   MM 33   ⌐Symphoniae sacrae. Pt.3, no.5⌐ O Herr, hilf. Cantata. Voices with instrumental ensemble. B.402.

1425   HAM 202   ⌐Symphoniae sacrae. Pt.3, no.18⌐ Saul, was verfolgst
       Nort3 17   du mich. 6 voices, 2 4-part choruses, and instrumental
ensemble. B.415.

1426   Hamb 52   SCHUYT, Cornelis, 1557-1616.
⌐Madrigals (1600) Dolce mia fiamma⌐ 5 voices.

Schwanke Nachtigall, 1453.

Schweiget mir vom Weibernehmen, 675, 1316.

1427	Amb 57f	SCOTUS, Paulus
		⌐Fallace speranza⌐ Frottola. 4 voices. Petrucci, Frottole, libro 8, fol.2.

Scutius, C see SCHUYT, Cornelis

Se ben or non scopro el focho, 1527.

Se bien fait, 1127.

Se cuer d'amant, 362.

Se j'ai, 825.

Se je souspir, 707.

Se la face ay pale, 479.

Se ne pas jeulx, 1144.

Se nel partir da voi, 1045.

Se nel sen di giovinetti, 309.

Se per colpa del vostro fiero sdegno, 84.

Se tu non m'ami, 25.

Se vostre ceur, 1145.

See, mine own sweet jewell, 1063.

Seelewig, 1453.

Sehet, Jesus hat die Hand, 119.

Seht, was die Liebe tut, 112.

Seht, wie Herr Elcius, 844.

1428	Ein 2	SEIKILOS, ca.1st cent.
	Flor 2a	⌐Hoson zes phainou⌐ Epitaph for the composer's wife,
	Glea 1	Euterpe.
	HAM 7c	
	Hamb 1	
	RMA 24	
	Scher 1	
	Starr 1	

Séjour de l'éternelle paix, 1299.

Seladons weltliche Lieder, 675.

1429	HAM 47	SELESSES, Jacopin, late 14th cent.
		⌐En attendant⌐ Ballade. 3 voices.

Selig sind die Toten, 1408.

Selva morale e spirituale, 1057.

1430	Amb 46	SENFL, Ludwig, 1492(ca.)-1555.
		⌐Ave rosa sine spinnis⌐ Motet. 5 voices. Tenor melody is Comme femme.
1431	HAM 110	⌐Da Jakob nu das Kleid ansah⌐ 4 voices.
1432	Scher 84	⌐Ewiger Gott⌐ Motet. 4 voices.
1433	Scher 86	⌐Fortuna⌐ 4 instruments.

1434 Min 69   ⌐Das Gläut zu Speyer¬ Lied. 6 voices.

1435 Amb 47b   ⌐Im Maien hört man die Hanen kreen¬ Lied. 4 voices.

1436 Flor 63   ⌐Mein freundlich's B.¬ Song. 4 voices.
       (For an arrangement for lute, see 1131)

1437 Wolf 28   ⌐Mein vleis und mus ich nie hab gspart¬ Lied.
4 voices.

1438 Scher 85   ⌐O Elslein¬ 2 voicés and 2 instruments.
Polytext: O Elslein; Es taget vor dem Walde.

1439 TEM 32   ⌐Oho, so geb' der Mann ein'n Pfenning¬ Polyphonic
Lied. 4 voices.

1440 Scher 76   ⌐Quis dabit oculis nostris¬ Ode on the death of Maxi-
milian I. 5 voices.

1441 HAM 109   ⌐Salutatio prima¬ Motet. 4 voices.

1442 Ein 14   ⌐Wol kumpt der May, voice and 3 instruments¬

1443 Amb 47a   ⌐Wol kumpt der May, 4 voices¬

Senleches, Jacques de. see SELESSES, Jacopin

Señor mio Jesu Cristo, 320.

Serà quel zorno, 1006.

1444 RR 59   SERMISY, Claude de, 1490(ca.)-1562.
⌐Jouissance vous donneray¬ Chanson. 4 voices.

1445 Lern 45   ⌐Pourtant si je suis brunette¬ Chanson. 4 voices.

Serse, 311.

Serva padrona, 1203-1204.

Serviteur, 1143, 1479.

Sfogava con le stelle, 268.

1446 OM 3b   Si ascendero in caelum Domine.
    RMA 22   Antiphon from the Office of the Dead. Mozarabic chant.

Si dolce non sonò, 898.

Si talor quella, 154.

Sia pur lodato il ciel, 1212.

Sie haben den Herren, 1409.

Sieben Worte Christi am Kreuz, 1418-1420.

Sicut cervus, 1183.

Silberweise, 1349.

Silva de sirenas, 1544.

Silver swan, 638.

Sing we and chant it, 1064.

Singende Muse an der Pleisse, 1405.

So wünsch ich ihr, 554.

Soeur Monique, 382.

Sok királ, 1510.

Sol oritur in sydere, 1217.

Solem, 825.

Soll, denn, schönste Doris, 35.

Solo e pensoso, 989.

Solomon, 734-735.

1447 Ein 32   SOMIS, Giovanni Battista, 1686-1763.
           ⌈Sonata, violin & continuo, D minor⌉ Reduced to two staves. Bass realized.

Sommeil, 1301.

Sommo Dio, 202.

Son si dolci le catene, 1378.

Sonata pian' e forte, 599.

Song of the ass, 1151.

1448 RMA 47   Song of the Sibyl.
           Cordovan version, 10th cent.

Song of sundry natures, 250-251.

Soupirs, 1303.

Souterliedekens, 347-348.

Soy contento y vos servido, 505.

Spanish paven, 228.

Speciosa facta es, 491.

Speciosus forma, 511.

Speme amorosa, 613.

Speranza, 165.

Speravi, 692.

Sperontes. see SCHOLZE, Johann Sigismund

1449 HAM 20a   SPERVOGEL, 12th cent.
           ⌈Swa eyn vriund⌉ Minnelied.

1450 Scher 63a   SPINACINO, Francesco, d.ca.1507.
           ⌈Intabolatura de lauto. La Bernardina⌉

1451 Scher 63b   ⌈Intabolatura de lauto. Ricercar, B-flat major⌉

1452 HAM 99b   ⌈Intabolatura de lauto. Ricercar, C major⌉

Spiritata, 593.

Splendida flamigero, 171.

Stabat mater, 271, 433, 1205.

1453 Scher 195 STADEN, Sigmund Theophil, 1607-1655.
           ⌈Seelewig. Die schwanke Nachtigall⌉ Aria with continuo, from the Singspiel.

1454 Wolf 31   STAHL, Joannes, 16th cent.
                   ⌐Ich will zu Land ausreiten⌐ Bicinium.

1455 Scher 305   STAMITZ, Johann Wenzel Anton, 1717-1757.
                   ⌐Sonata da camera, violin & continuo, op.6, no.2,
                   C major. Adagio⌐

1456 HAM 294   ⌐Symphony, op.5, no.2, D Major. Presto⌐ First move-
                   ment.

1457 Flor 173   ⌐Trio-sonata, op.1, no.1, C major. Allegro⌐

1458 Scher 309a STANDFUSS, Johann C   d.ca.1759.
                   ⌐Die verwandelten Weiber. Es war einmal ein junge Weib⌐
                   Song from the Singspiel (alternate title: Der Teufel ist
                   los) With keyboard.

                   Stantipes. see Estampie

1459 Wolf 21   STAPPEN, Crispinus van, 1470?-1532 or 3.
                   ⌐Vale de Padoa⌐ Frottola (strambotto) 3 voices.

                   Stay, cruel, stay, 403.

1460 HAM 244   STEFFANI, Agostino, 1654-1728.
                   ⌐Henrico Leone. Un balen⌐ Da capo aria.

1461 Hamb 59   ⌐Lontananza crudel⌐ Chamber duet. 2 voices with con-
                   tinuo.

1462 Scher 242   ⌐Occhi, perchè piangete⌐ Cantata. Soprano and alto
                   with continuo.

1463 Ein 30   ⌐Orlando generoso. Overture⌐ French overture. Key-
                   board score.

1464 OM 83   Stella splendens.
                   Polyphonic pilgrim song with tornada. Spanish, 14th
                   cent. 2 voices.

                   Stirpe Maria, 1111.

1465 Glea 33   Stirps Jesse florigeram.
                   Organum. Trope on Benedicamus Domino. Early 12th cent.
                   2 voices. Incomplete. St. Martial school.

                   Stirps Mocenigo, 80.

                   Stizzoso mio stizzoso, 1204.

1466 HAM 108   STOLTZER, Thomas, 1480(ca.)-1526.
                   ⌐Christ ist erstanden⌐ Hymn. 4 voices.

1467 Amb 36   ⌐Hilff Herr, die Heylligen⌐ Psalm 12. 6 voices.

                   Strada, 1012.

1468 HAM 241   STRADELLA, Alessandro, 1644-1682.
                   ⌐Il corispero. Trà cruci funesti⌐ Aria from act 2,
                   scene 14. With instrumental ensemble.

1469 Scher 229   ⌐Sinfonia, violin, violoncello & continuo, D minor⌐
                   Suite.

1470 Scher 230   ⌐Susanna. Da chi spero⌐ Aria, with instrumental en-
                   semble.

Stravaganze d'amore, 985.

1471 Flor 31   Sumer is icumen in.
      Glea 45   English round, ca.1310. 4 voices and pes I and II.
      HAM 42
      Scher 17
      Starr 17

Super flumina Babylonis, 662.

Sur le ioly ionc, 1625.

Surrexit Christus hodie, 183.

Sus une fontayne, 343.

Susanna, 1470.

Susanne un jour, 590, 918

1472 SS 8   SUSATO, Tylman, fl.1529-1561, compiler.
                     ⌐Danserye. Selections⌐ La mourisque. Pavane, La
                     bataille. Dances. 4 instruments.

1473 Scher 119   ⌐Musyck boexken, no.3. Selections⌐ Ronde and Salta-
                     rello. 4 instruments.

1474 Lern 48   ⌐Musyck boexken, no.3. Pavane-gaillarde, Mille ducas⌐
                     4 instruments.

Suspiro, 709.

Swa eyn vriund, 1449.

Sweelinck, Jan Pieterszoon. see SWELINCK, JP

Sweet echo, 924.

1475 HAM 181   SWELINCK, Jan Pietersz., 1562-1621.
                     ⌐Echo fantasia, keyboard instrument⌐

1476 Flor 107   ⌐Fantasia, organ, D major⌐

1477 Hamb 83   ⌐Fantasia chromatica, organ⌐
      Scher 158
      Starr 98

1478 Hamb 64   ⌐Psaumes de David. Tu as esté, Seigneur⌐ Psalm 90.
                     4 voices.

Symphoniae sacrae, 1421-1425.

Tabulaturen etlicher Lobgesang, 1400-1401.

1479 Scher 68   TADINGHEN, Jakob, fl.ca.1500.
                     ⌐Le serviteur⌐ Chanson. 2 instruments.

Taeggio. see ROGNONI, Giovanni Domenico

Tag des Gerichts, 1495.

1480 RMA 99   Talent mes prus.
                     Canon. 14th cent. 2 voices.

1481 HAM 127   TALLIS, Thomas, 1505(ca.)-1585.
                     ⌐Audivi vocem⌐ Responsorium (motet) 4 voices.

1482 Scher 129 ⌐Cantiones sacrae (1575) In manus tuas⌐ Motet.
5 voices. From Psalm 31.

1483 Flor 79 ⌐Cantiones sacrae (1575) Salvator mundi⌐ Motet.
5 voices.

1484 TEM 27 ⌐Hear the voice and prayer⌐ Anthem. 4 voices.

Tambourin, 1304.

1485 OM 33 TANNHÄUSER, 1200(ca.)-1266.
⌐Ez ist hiute eyn wunnychlicher tac⌐ Minnelied.
Spruchdichtung in bar form.

Tant con je vivrai, 18.

Tant doulcement, 708.

Tant mes plazens, 716.

Tanti strali al sen, 721.

1486 HAM 85 Tappster, dryngker.
Min 80 Song. English, ca.1475. 3 voices.

1487 Scher 295 TARTINI, Giuseppe, 1692-1770.
⌐Pastorale, violin & continuo, A major. Selections⌐
Grave and Allegro.

1488 Flor 164 ⌐Sonata, violin & continuo, op.1, no.1, A major. Grave⌐
1st movement.

1489 HAM 275 ⌐Sonata, violin & continuo, op.3, no.12, G major.
Presto⌐

1490 HAM 112 TAVERNER, John, 1495(ca.)-1545.
⌐Mass, The western wynde. Benedictus⌐ 4 voices. Includes the original tune.

Te Deum laudamus, 1406.

Te martyrum, 62.

Teco, signora mia, 39.

1491 Lern 6 Tecum principium.
Gradual. Gregorian chant.

1492 Flor 156 TELEMANN, Georg Philipp, 1681-1767.
⌐Fantasia, harpsichord, D minor⌐

1493 TEM 48 ⌐Fantasia, violin, no.4, D major⌐

1494 HAM 271 ⌐Quartets, flute, strings & continuo (1730) Sonata 1.
Soave⌐ 1st movement of the 3d Paris quartet (A major).

1495 HAM 272 ⌐Der Tag des Gerichts. Chor der Seligen⌐ 4 voices,
with instrumental ensemble.

1496 Scher 299 ⌐Die vergesserne Phyllis⌐ Song. With continuo.

1497 Scher 266 ⌐Was ist schöner als die Liebe⌐ Aria from an unknown
opera. With instrumental ensemble.

1498 Flor 157 ⌐Werfet Panier auf im Lande⌐ Motet. 4 voices.

Telus purpurium, 171.

Temple de la gloire, 1307.

Tempo fuge, 306.

Ténébreuse, 378.

Ter terni sunt modi, 766.

Terpsichore, 1266-1267.

Terradeglias, Domenico. see TERRADELLAS, Domingo...

1499 HAM 298 TERRADELLAS, Domingo Miguel Bernabé, 1713-1751.
⌐In vasto mare infido¬ Motet. Solo voice with instrumental ensemble.

1500 Scher 298 ⌐Merope. Figlio, ascolta¬ Recitative and aria, act 3, scene 2. With orchestra.

Teufel ist los, 1458.

1501 Scher 210 THEILE, Johann, 1646-1724.
⌐Durchkläre dich, du Silbernacht¬ Aria. With instrumental ensemble. From his Weltliche Arien und Canzonetten, 1667.

Theios thesauros, 1503.

1502 Scher VII THEODOROS Studites, 759-826.
⌐Tokatharontes hagneias su chrema¬ Greek chant. Hymne zum Gedächtnis der Heiligen Euphrosyne.

1503 Scher VIII ⌐Theios thesauros¬ Greek chant. Hymne zum Feste der Kreuzerhöhung.

1504 OM 26 THIBAUT IV, King of Navarre, 1201-1253.
⌐Dame, merci¬ Trouvère jeu-parti.

1505 OM 25 ⌐Dex est ausi comme li pellicans¬ Trouvère sirventois, vers form.

1506 Flor 16b ⌐En chantant vueil ma dolor descouvrir¬ Trouvère song.

1507 RMA 54 ⌐Por conforter ma pesance¬ Trouvère ballade.

1508 Scher 13 ⌐Pour ce se d'amer me dueil¬ Trouvère song.

This is the record of John, 641.

Thy hand, Belinda, 1276.

Thyrsis, sleepest thou? 172.

Ti lascio l'alma impegno, 938.

Tich, tach, toch, 1548.

1509 Wolf 15 TINCTORIS, Jean, d.1511.
⌐Virgo Dei throno digna¬ Motet. 3 voices.

1510 RR 163 TINÓDI, Sebestyén, 1510(ca.)-1556.
⌐Sok kiráról, császárról emléköztem¬ Song. Emperor Soliman's fight with Kazul Pasha (1546).

Tisbe, si può haver pietà, 1371.

1511 HAM 180 TITELOUZE, Jean, 1563-1633.
⌐Pange lingua, organ¬

Tod Jesu, 672.

Todtkrancke und wieder gesunde Hiskias, 872.

Tokatharontes hagneias su chrema, 1502.

Tolomeo, 738.

Tombeau de Mlle. Gaultier, 620.

Tombeau de Mons. de Lenclos, 621.

1512 HAM 176 TOMKINS, Thomas, 1572-1656.
⌐In nomine, 3 viols⌐

1513 HAM 169 ⌐Songs of 3, 4, 5, and 6 parts. No.19⌐ When David
heard. Anthem. 5 voices.

Ton corps qui de bien amer, 709.

Torcia, 204.

1514 Hamb 90 TORELLI, Giuseppe, 1658-1709.
⌐Concerto grosso, op.8, no.5, G major⌐

1515 Scher 257 ⌐Concerto grosso, op.8, no.7, D minor⌐

1516 HAM 246 ⌐Concerto grosso, op.8, no.8, C minor. Last movement⌐

1517 Flor 142 ⌐Trio-sonata, violin, violoncello & continuo, D major.
Allegro⌐

1518 HAM 102a TORRE, Francisco de la, fl.1483-1502.
⌐Alta⌐ Basse danse. 3 instruments.

Tortorella, 1128.

Tosto che l'alba, 633.

Tota pulchra es, 27.

Tourbillons, 1305.

Tournai mass, 1035-1036.

Tous les regretz, 906.

1519 Starr 19 Toutes voies.
Motet. 13th cent. 3 voices. Polytext: Toutes voies;
Trop ai de grieté; Je la truis.

Tra cruci funesti, 1468.

1520 HAM 191 TRABACI, Giovanni Maria, 1580(ca.)-1647.
⌐Ricercate, canzone francese, capricci... libro 1.
No.6⌐ Canzona francese, keyboard instrument.

1521 OM 72 Tres dous compains.
Chace. French, mid-14th cent. 3 voices.

1522 RMA 56 TRESORIERS de Lille, 13th c.
⌐Haut honor d'un commandement⌐ Trouvère hymn (vers).

Tri ciechi siamo povr' inamorati, 1103.

Triste plaisir, 191.

Tristis est anima mea, 919.

1523 Scher 73   TRITONIUS, Petrus, 15th-16th cent.
                  [Melopoiae sive harmoniae tetracenticae (1507) Vides
                  ut alta stet] 4 voices.

                Triumph of time and truth, 740.

1524 Scher 69   TROMBONCINO, Bartolomeo, fl.1487-1514.
                  [Benche amor mi faccia] Frottola. Voice and 3 instru-
                  ments.

1525 RR 32   [Io son l'ocello che non pò volare] Frottola. 4
                  voices.

1526 HAM 95a   [Non val aqua] Frottola. 4 voices.

1527 Wolf 22   [Se ben or non scopro el focho] Frottola. 4 voices.

                Trop ai de grieté, 1519.

                Trop plus est belle, 710.

1528 HAM 32d   Trop sovent.
      Glea 62   Motet. 13th cent. 3 voices. Polytext: Trop sovent;
                  Brunete; In seculum.

1529 Glea 57   Trotto.
                  English dance, 14th cent. 1 instrument.

                Tsaat een meskin, 1129.

                Tu as esté, Seigneur, 1478.

1530 Flor 20   Tu patris.
                  Organum. 9th cent.

                Tu pauperum refugium, 434.

                Tu sei morta, 1054.

1531 Scher 211   TUNDER, Franz, 1614-1667.
                  [Ein kleines Kindelein] Aria. With strings and organ.

1532 HAM 215   [Prelude and fugue, organ, G minor]

1533 HAM 214   [Wachet auf, ruft uns die Stimme. Wachet auf] Aria.
                  With instrumental ensemble.

1534 Flor 10   TUOTILO, d.915.
      Scher 3   [Hodie cantandus est] Christmas trope to the introit
                  of the Missa in nativitate Domini. Incomplete.

1535 HAM 15b   [Omnipotens genitor] Kyrie trope, to Missa Cunctipotens.

1536 Scher 133   TURNHOUT, Gérard de, 1520(ca.)-1580.
                  [En regardant] Canonic chanson. 2 voices.

1537 Flor 3   Tús forsíras tús megálus tís ekklisías.
                  Byzantine chant. 13th cent.

                Tutilo. see TUOTILO

1538 RMA 73   Tvisöngur [i.e., Two-part song]
                  Organum. Icelandic, 790.

1539 RR 185   TYE, Christopher, 1497?-1572.
                  [The actes of the Apostles. Chapter 10] 4 voices.

Uccel di Dio, 815.

Ulisse troppo errò, 1055.

Under der linden, 1603.

Ungarescha, 1168.

Unschuldiger Ritter, 779.

Uss... see Aus...

Ut heremita solus, 1146.

1540 RMA 30   Ut queant laxis.
    Hymn. Gregorian chant. Used by Guido d'Arezzo to
    establish names for scale degrees.

Ut queant laxis, 192, 1540.

1541 Flor 130   Ut-re-mi-fa-sol-la.
    Catch. English, 17th cent. 5 voices.

1542 Glea 29   Ut tuo propitiatus.
  HAM 26b   Free organum. 1th cent. 2 voices.

Vaghe stelle, 307.

1543 Lern 30   VAILLANT, Jean, 14th cent.
    ⌜Par maintes foys⌝ Virelai. 3 voices.

Vaiyicra moshe... see Wayiqra moshe...

1544 HAM 124   VALDERRÁBANO, Enríquez de, 1500-1557.
    ⌜Silva de sirenas. Guardame las vacas⌝ Variations.
    Lute.

Vale de Padoa, 1459.

Varii fiori del giardino musicale, 203.

Vater unser im Himmelreich, 129, 242, 1165, 1264, 1390.

1545 Flor 96   VECCHI, Orazio, 1550-1605.
    ⌜L'Amfiparnaso. Hor per vegnir⌝ Chorus from act 1,
    scene 3. Incomplete.

1546 Hamb 57   ⌜L'Amfiparnaso. Misero che farò⌝ Chorus from act 2,
    scene 1. 5 voices.

1547 Scher 164   ⌜L'Amfiparnaso. O pierulin dov' estu?⌝ From act 1,
    scene 1. Soloists with chorus.

1548 Lern 59   ⌜L'Amfiparnaso. Tich, tach, toch⌝ Chorus from act 3,
    scene 3. 5 voices.

1549 Glea 8   Veine pleine.
    Trouvère song. Strophic laisse. Late 13th cent.

Velut stellae firmamenti, 786.

Venetus, Franciscus. see ANA, Francesco d'

1550 TEM 4   Veni creator spiritus.
    Hymn for the second Vespers of Whitsunday. Gregorian
    chant.

Veni creator spiritus, 193, 482, 541, 1550.

Veni de libano, 1421.

1551 TEM 41   Veni redemptor gentium.
     Gregorian hymn.

Veni redemptor gentium, 65, 1312, 1551.

1552 Flor 14   Veni sancte spiritus.
     Conductus. 12th cent.

1553 Flor 13   Veni sancte spiritus.
   Lern 9   Whitsuntide sequence, ca.1020.
   Scher 5

Veni sancte spiritus, 492, 541, 1550, 1552-1553.

Veni sponsa Christi, 1181.

1554 RMA 60   Venite a laudare.
     Italian lauda, 13th cent.

Venus and Adonis, 196.

Venus, du und dein Kind, 1313.

Venus Kräntzlein, 1398.

1555 Glea 35   Verbum bonum et suave.
   Scher 10 Organum, conductus style. 13th cent. Polyphonic se-
     quence. 2 voices.

Verbum caro, 1355.

Verbum iniquum, 531.

1556 Scher 97   VERDELOT, Philippe, d.ca.1550.
     [Ave sanctissima] Canon in diatessaron. 6 voices.
     From the 3d book of motets, 1534. B.pt.2,I, Motet 11.

1557 Scher 98   [Madonna, per voi ardo] Madrigal. 4 voices. From
     the 1st book of madrigals, 1533. B.pt.2,II,61.

Vergesserne Phyllis, 1496.

1558 Wolf 37   Vergine bella che di solvestita.
     Lauda. 16th cent. 2 voices.

Vergine pura, 1332.

1559 Glea 44   Veri floris sub figura.
   Starr 19 Conductus. Vers. Spanish, 13th cent. 3 voices.

1560 Glea 41   Veris ad imperia.
     Conductus. Easter hymn. Early 13th cent. Notre Dame
     school.

Veritatem, 333, 1355.

1561 OM 101   Verlangen thut mich krencken.
     Monophonic Lied. German, ca.1450.

Verwandelten Weiber, 1458.

Vesconta, 1011.

Vespro della Beata Vergine, 1058.

1562 Flor 7   Vexilla regis prodeunt.
                 Hymn. Gregorian chant.

1563 Wolf 52   VIADANA, Lodovico da, 1564-1645.
                 ⌜Centum sacri concentus. O dulcissima Maria⌝ Voice
                 and continuo.

1564 Flor 109 ⌜Concerti ecclesiastici. Decantabat populus Israel⌝
                 Voice and continuo.

1565 HAM 185   ⌜Concerti ecclesiastici. Exaudi me, Domine⌝ Voice and
                 continuo.

1566 Lern 61   ⌜Concerti ecclesiastici. O Domine Jesu Christe⌝ Voice
                 and continuo.

1567 Scher 168 ⌜Concerti ecclesiastici, op.12. Salve regina⌝ Motet.
                 2 voices with continuo.

                 Victimae paschali laudes, 344, 833, 1626-1627.

1568 Flor 90   VICTORIA, Tomás Luis de, 1548(ca.)-1611.
                 ⌜Jesus redemptor omnium⌝ Motet. 4 voices. Original
                 Gregorian hymn included. From his Hymni totius anni
                 (1585)

1569 Lern 52   ⌜Missa, O magnum mysterium. Sanctus⌝ 4 voices.

1570 Lern 51   ⌜O magnum mysterium⌝ Motet. 4 voices.

1571 Scher 128 ⌜O magnum mysterium. Part 1⌝ Motet. 4 voices.

1572 HAM 149   ⌜O vos omnes⌝ Motet. 4 voices.

                 Viderunt, 1218.

1573 Glea 32   Viderunt Hemanuel.
      HAM 27a   Melismatic organum. ca.1125. 2 voices. St. Martial
                 school.

                 Viderunt omnes, 951.

                 Vides ut alta stet, 1523.

1574 MM 2   Vidimus stellam.
                 Alleluia. Gregorian chant. From the Mass for Epiphany.

                 Viel schöner Blümelein, 1395.

                 Vierge pucelle, 929.

                 Violetta, 1056.

                 Virgine matre, 914.

                 Virgo Dei throno digna, 1509.

                 Virgo Maria, 272, 1615.

                 Virgo prudentissima, 805, 813.

                 Virgo virginum, 1290.

                 Virtuose, 1201.

1575 Flor 138 VITALI, Giovanni Battista, 1632-1692.
                 ⌜Capriccio, 4 strings, F minor⌝ In five sections.

1576 HAM 245   ⌐Sonatas, op.5. No.5⌐ La graziani. Trio-sonata.
                   Violins and continuo.

1577 HAM 263   VITALI, Tommaso Antonio, 1663-1745.
                   ⌐Trio-sonata, op.1, no.4, D minor⌐

1578 Scher 241   ⌐Trio-sonata, op.2, no.5, B minor⌐

1579 Scher 88a   Vitrum nostrum gloriosum.
                   Drinking song. German, ca.1540. 4 voices.

                   Vittrici schieri, 1361.

                   Viva sempre in ogni etate, 449.

1580 Flor 154   VIVALDI, Antonio, 1678-1741.
                   ⌐La cetra. No.3. 1st movement⌐ Violin concerto,
                   op.9, no.3, G minor.

1581 TEM 47   ⌐Il cimento dell'armonia e dell'invenzione. No.1. Al-
                   legro⌐ 1st movement of the violin concerto op.8, no.1,
                   E major (La primavera).

1582 Scher 276   ⌐Il cimento dell'armonia e dell'inventione. No.1.
                   Largo⌐ 2d movement of the violin concerto op.8, no.1,
                   E major (La primavera).

1583 SS 38   ⌐Il cimento dell'armonia e dell'invenzione. No.3⌐
                   Violin concerto, op.8, no.3, F major (L'autumno).

1584 Lern 77   ⌐L'estro armonico. No.2⌐ Concerto grosso op.3, no.2,
                   for strings and continuo.

1585 HAM 270   ⌐L'estro armonico. No.6. Allegro⌐ 1st movement of
                   the concerto grosso op.3, no.6, for strings and con-
                   tinuo.

1586 Nort3 20   ⌐L'estro armonico. No.11⌐ Concerto grosso, op.3,
                   no.11, for strings and continuo.

1587 Flor 155   ⌐Magnificat. Quia fecit mihi magna⌐ Aria, from the
                   second version. With instrumental ensemble.

                   Vive le roy, 435.

                   Viver lieto voglio, 614.

                   Vogelweide, Walther von der. see WALTHER von der Vogel-
                       weide

                   Voglio morir, 1043.

                   Voi mi ponest' in foco, 85.

                   Voi ve n'andat' al cielo, 86.

                   Volunté, 624.

                   Vom Himmel hoch, 1166, 1265.

                   Von edler art, 1402.

                   Vor deinen Thron tret' ich, 137.

                   Vorjahrslied, 36.

Vorria che tu cantass', 1365.

Vos n'aler, 689.

Vos qui admiramini, 1233.

Vos qui paretix, 402.

1588 Glea 2   Voskresenie mvoi Khrïsme.
                 Russian chant. 11th cent.

1589 RMA 13   Voskriesni Gospodi, pomdzi nam.
                 Russian Znamenny chant, 17th cent,

                Vous me tuez, 1008.

                Vox in Rama audita est, 349.

                Vrolick en bly loeft god, 348.

                Wach auf, du werte Christenheit, 495.

                Wach auff, myn hort, 1631.

                Wachet auf, 138, 1533.

                Wacht auff ir werden christen, 1350.

1590 Scher 45 Wald hat sich entlaubet.
                 Song. German, ca.1450. 3 voices.

1591 Amb 56   WALLISER, Christoph Thomas, 1568-1648.
                 ⌐Deus noster refugium. German⌐ Psalm 46. Motet.
                 5 voices. Based on the music and text of the chorale
                 Ein' feste Burg ist unser Gott. From his Ecclesiociae,
                 1614.

1592 Scher 81 WALTHER, Johann, 1496-1570.
                 ⌐Fugen auff acht Tonos. Canon, 3 instruments⌐

1593 HAM 111a ⌐Geystliche gesangk Buchleyn. Aus tiefer Not⌐ Chorale.
                 4 voices.

1594 Flor 66   ⌐Geystliche gesangk Buchleyn. Christ lag in Todes-
                 banden⌐ Chorale. 4 voices.
                   (Not the same setting as Scher 80)

1595 Scher 80 ⌐Geystliche gesangk Buchleyn. Christ lag in Todes-
                 bandan⌐ Motet. 4 voices.
                   (Not the same setting as Flor 66)

1596 Lern 43-44 ⌐Geystliche gesangk Buchleyn. Gelobet seist du, Jesu
                 Christ⌐ Chorale. 4 voices. 2 settings.

1597 TEM 24   ⌐Geystliche gesangk Buchleyn. Komm, Gott Schöpfer,
                 heiliger Geist⌐ Chorale. 4 voices.

1598 Amb 48   ⌐Holdseliger meins Hertzen Trost⌐ Motet. 6 voices.
                 ca.1566.

1599 Amb 48b   ⌐Ein newes christliches Lied⌐ 4 voices.
      Wolf 35

1600 Scher 291 WALTHER, Johann Gottfried, 1684-1748.
                 ⌐Wie soll ich dich empfangen, organ. Verses 2, 8, 9⌐
                 Chorale variations.

1601 Scher 239 WALTHER, Johann Jakob, 1650-1717.
                 ⌐Scherzi da violino solo con il basso continuo. Suite,
                 no.1, A major. Selections⌐ Sarabande and gigue.

1602 Flor 17a   WALTHER von der Vogelweide, d.ca.1230.
      Glea 20   ⌐Palästinalied⌐ Nu al'erst. Minnelied (bar).
      HAM 20b
      Hamb 9
      RMA 57
      Scher 12

1603 OM 31   ⌐Under der linden⌐ Minnelied.

1604 Scher 12   ⌐Wie sol ich den gemynnen⌐ Minnelied.

                  Walter, Johann, 1496-1570. see WALTHER, Johann, 1496-1570

                  Wann unsre Augen schlafen ein, 1411.

                  Warum betrübst du dich, 1391.

                  Was hast du verwirket, 1412.

                  Was ist schöner als die Liebe, 1497.

1605 HAM 6a-b   Wayiqra moshe l'khol ziqne Yisrael.
                     Jewish chant. Syrian intonation of the Pentateuch.
                     Includes the Syrian Ta'amim (accents)

1606 Flor 1   Wayiqra moshe l'khol ziqne Yisrael.
                     Jewish chant. Two intonations from the Pentateuch.

                  Wê, ich han gedacht, 1629.

1607 HAM 102b   WECK, Hans, 1495(ca.)-1536.
                     ⌐Spanyöler Tancz, instruments⌐ Solo line with chordal
                     accompaniment. Includes a Hopper dancz.

1608 Scher 213a WECKMANN, Matthias, 1621-1674.
                     ⌐Weine nicht. Sinfonia⌐ Overture. 6 strings and
                     organ.

1609 Scher 212   ⌐Wenn der Herr die Gefangenen zu Zion. Die mit Tränen
                  säen⌐ 4-part chorus from the cantata. With instrumen-
                  tal ensemble.

1610 Min 84   WEELKES, Thomas, 1575(ca.)-1623.
                     ⌐Airs, 3-6 part. The ape, the monkey, and the baboon⌐
                     3 voices.

1611 Nort3 16   ⌐As Vesta was descending⌐ Madrigal. 6 voices. From
                  Morley's The triumphs of Oriana.

1612 HAM 170   ⌐Balletts and madrigals (1598) Hark, all ye lovely
                  saints⌐ Ballett. 5 voices.

1613 RR 213   ⌐For 2 basses⌐ Fantasia for 6 strings.

1614 Scher 58   WEERBECKE, Gaspar von, 1440(ca.)-1514.
                     ⌐Lamentationes Jeremiae prophetae, book 2. Incipit la-
                     mentatio⌐ Motet. 4 voices.

1615 Amb 24   ⌐Virgo Maria⌐ Motet. 4 voices.

                  Wehe, Windgen, wehe, 1392.

Weil dann so unstet, 931.

Wein, der schmeckt mir also wol, 1366.

Weine nicht, 1608.

1616 Lern 82   WEISS, Sylvius Leopold, 1686-1750.
                      ⌈Fantasia, lute, E-flat major⌉

Wende Dich, Herr, 741.

Wenn der Herr die Gefangegen zu Zion, 1609.

Wenn ich einmal soll scheiden, 119.

Wenn ich, O Schöpfer, deine Macht, 97.

Wenn wir in höchsten Nöthen sein, 130.

Wer ·sehen will zween lebendige Brunnen, 1314.

Werfet Panier auf im Lande, 1498.

Wer's Jagen recht begreifen will, 867.

1617 HAM 146a   WERT, Giaches de, 1535-1596.
                      ⌈Madrigals, book 1. Cara la vita⌉ 5 voices.

Werth, Jacob von. see WERT, Giaches de

Western wynde, 1490.

Weyber mit den Flöhen, 1131.

What if I never speed, 456.

When David heard, 1513.

When I am laid in earth, 1276.

When Laura smiles, 1337.

Who is like unto Thee, 723.

1618 Scher 186   WIDMANN, Erasmus, 1572-1634.
                      ⌈Musicalischer Studentenmuht. No.1⌉ Kompt, her, ihr
                      Herrn. Student song. 4 voices.

Wie sol ich den gemynnen, 1604.

Wie soll ich dich empfangen, 1600.

1619 Flor 58   WILLAERT, Adrian, 1490?-1562.
                      ⌈O dolce vita mia⌉ Canzon villanesca. 4 voices.

1620 Ein 15   ⌈O magnum mysterium. Part 1⌉ Motet. 4 voices.

1621 Scher 104   ⌈O salutaris hostia⌉ Canonic motet. 2 voices and 4
                       instruments.

1622 Amb 58   ⌈Pater noster⌉ Motet. 4 voices.
      Hamb 46

1623 HAM 115   ⌈Ricercari a tre voci. Ricercar⌉ 3 instruments.
                       Ricercar no.10 of his Fantasie, recercari contrapunti
                       (1559).

1624 Scher 105   ⌈Ricercari a tre voci. Ricercar⌉ 3 instruments. From
                       Motetti trium vocum (ca.1552).

| 1625 | Wolf 27 | ⌐Sur le ioly ionc⌐ Polyphonic chanson. 3 voices. |
| 1626 | HAM 113 | ⌐Victimae paschali laudes⌐ Motet. 6 voices. From Musica nova. |

Willekommen mayenschein, 1092.

Willst du dein Herz mir schenken, 122.

Winder wie ist, 1093.

| 1627 | Flor 12
HAM 16b
Hamb 5
MM 3
RMA 42
Scher 6 | WIPO, ca.995-1050.
⌐Victimae paschali laudes⌐ Easter sequence. Gregorian. |

Wir essen und leben wohl, 107.

With drooping wings, 1277.

Witzlav. see WIZLAW von Rügen

| 1628 | OM 35 | WIZLAW von Rügen, d.1325.
⌐Ich warne dich⌐ Spruch, bar form. Minnelied. |
| 1629 | Glea 20 | ⌐Wê, ich han gedacht⌐ Minnelied. |

Wohltemperierte Clavier, 139-142.

Wohnt noch Mitlied, 1407.

Wol kumpt der May, 1442-1443.

1630	HAM 60	WOLKENSTEIN, Oswald von, 1277?-1445. ⌐Der May⌐ Minnelied. Voice and instrument.
1631	Flor 39 RMA 120 Scher 46	⌐Wach auff, myn hort⌐ Minnelied. 2 voices, or voice with instrument.
1632	HAM 23b Starr 14	Worldes blis. English song, 13th cent. 1 voice.

Xerxes, 970.

Yeger horn, 651.

Zabaione musicale, 150.

Zart schöne Jungfräulein, 556.

Zefiro torna, 1048.

| 1633 | Amb 57e | ZESSO, Giovanni Battista.
⌐E quando andarete⌐ Frottola. 4 voices. Petrucci, Frottole, libro 7, fol.55. |

Zwischen Berg und tiefem Tal, 814.

Part 2: SUBJECTS

Part 2: SUBJECTS

Numerical references are to the item numbers of entries
in Part 1; verbal references are to other subjects.

Airs. see Part-songs, Secular, English; Songs, Secular, English

Albas; Aubes
   605, 715.

Allemandes
   63, 146, 200, 211, 329, 378-379, 574, 625, 1231.

Anthems
   195, 249-250, 390, 636, 639, 641, 674, 784, 1281, 1484, 1513.

Arias
      Includes excerpts from large works.
   CAVALLI: 307-309, 311. CESTI: 323-324, 326. HÄNDEL: 721-722, 724-725,
   728, 730-731, 733, 738, 740. HILLER: 768-770. KEISER: 841-846.
   LULLY: 961-962, 964, 967-968. MONTEVERDI: 1041-1042, 1044, 1049,
   1052-1053, 1055. PEPUSCH: 1195-1198. PERGOLESI: 1200-1205.
   H PURCELL: 1274, 1276, 1278, 1282. RAMEAU: 1298-1299, 1307.
   OTHER: 7, 25, 87, 112, 119, 201-202, 235, 261, 271, 281, 292, 294, 302,
   377, 509-510, 583, 602, 607-608, 671, 748, 866-867, 875, 885, 924, 938,
   952, 960, 985, 1007, 1210-1211, 1239, 1269, 1338, 1341, 1361, 1371, 1378,
   1407, 1409, 1453, 1460, 1468, 1470, 1497, 1500-1501, 1531, 1533, 1587.
      see also Songs, Secular

Aubes. see Albas

Ballades
   TROUBADOUR: 1. TROUVÈRE: 9, 15, 507, 829, 1082, 1219, 1222, 1507.
   14th CENT.: 693, 696-697, 699, 706, 958, 1429.
   15th CENT.: 79, 187, 480, 678.

Ballate
   69, 644, 886-889, 894-895, 897, 1006.

Balletti
   450, 610-614.

Balletts. see Part-songs, Secular, English

Basses danses
   155-157, 624, 683, 1518.

Branles
   212, 1231, 1267.

Cacce. see Canons

Canons, Instrumental
   121, 203, 411, 435, 1592.
      see also Fugues

Canons, Vocal
   14th CENT.: 633, 643, 706, 890, 1099-1100, 1119, 1147, 1240, 1471,
   1480, 1521. 15th-EARLY 16th CENT.: 414, 424, 900, 1074, 1556.
   MID-16th-17th CENT.: 215, 374, 496, 584, 1086, 1280, 1536, 1541.
      see also Fugues, Vocal

Cansos
   173, 177, 1326.

Cantatas: for single excerpts, see Arias; Chorales;
         Choruses; Overtures; Recitatives

Cantatas, Sacred
   109, 113, 138, 284, 1397, 1411-1412, 1421-1422, 1424.

Cantatas, Secular
   600, 1372, 1375, 1379, 1462.

Canzoni (Harpsichord)
   283, 358, 566-567, 588, 590.

Canzoni (Instrumental ensemble)
   415, 532, 592-593, 802-803, 810, 824, 975, 999, 1012, 1129, 1327,
   1433, 1479.

Canzoni (Organ)
   232, 314, 560, 810, 1013.

Carols
   410, 1010, 1114, 1262, 1351.

Catches. see Canons

Chaconnes. see Variations

Chamber music. see Instrumental ensembles; Sonatas; Suites; Trio-sonatas

Chansons. see Songs, Secular, French

Chansons, Polyphonic
   AGRICOLA: 27-29. DEPRÈS: 412, 414, 416, 418, 421-422, 431. JANEQUIN:
   821-823. LASSUS: 908, 917-918. OBRECHT: 1121, 1127, 1130. OCKEGHEM:
   1133-1134, 1144-1145. OTHER: 83, 184, 188, 229, 269, 321-322, 352, 376,
   387, 467, 471, 486-487, 634, 820, 828, 942, 1073, 1444-1445, 1625.

Chansons mesurées
   943-944, 1008.

Chants, Ambrosian
   3, 20, 22, 50, 95, 441, 511, 835, 1292, 1310.

Chants, Byzantine
   514, 785, 832, 838, 1236, 1249, 1308, 1330, 1537.

Chants, Gallican
   392, 1252.

Chants, Greek
   1502-1503.
      see also Songs, Greek

Chants, Gregorian
   MODES: 676. AGNUS: 23. ALLELUIA: 51-53, 55-56, 61, 1106, 1574.
   ANTIPHON: 88, 162, 407, 765, 788, 920, 923, 1108. BENEDICAMUS: 167.
   COLLECT: 440. CREDO: 389. EPISTLE: 291. GLORIA: 652, 1000.
   GRADUAL: 511, 719, 1292, 1491. HYMN: 21, 339, 1185, 1322, 1540,
   1550-1551, 1562, 1568. INTROIT: 447, 616. KYRIE: 394, 876-880, 1001,
   1032. LITURGICAL DRAMA: 796.   (Continued on next page)

Chants, Gregorian (cont.)
  MASS: 298-300, 1034. OFFERTORY: 834. PSALM: 88, 162, 393, 788, 920-921.
  RESPONSORY: 773, 953. SANCTUS: 1000, 1358. TRACT: 1291.
    see also Conductus; Organa; Sequences; Tropes

Chants, Hindu
  758.

Chants, Jewish
  836, 936, 1605-1606.

Chants, Mozarabic
  438-439, 617, 1317, 1446.

Chants, Russian
  1251, 1588-1589.

Chants, Syrian
  839, 1605.

Chorale preludes
  JS BACH: 110, 123, 125-130, 137. BUXTEHUDE: 234, 236-238, 242.
  J PACHELBEL: 1158-1159, 1161, 1165-1166. OTHER: 199, 225, 537,
  853, 855, 857, 1390.

Chorales
    Includes excerpts from large works.
  JS BACH: 107, 114, 118-119, 124. Johann WALTHER: 1593-1594, 1596-1597.
  OTHER: 216, 273, 338, 945, 971, 980, 1024, 1155-1157, 1264.

Choruses: includes excerpts from large works.
    see also Hymns; Motets; Part-songs, Sacred;
            Part-songs, Secular; Psalms

Choruses, Sacred
  HÄNDEL: 723, 726-727, 734-735. OTHER: 106, 233, 235, 271, 292, 295, 623,
  672, 752, 930, 1058, 1126, 1283, 1396, 1406, 1420, 1425, 1495, 1609.

Choruses, Secular
  196, 325, 603, 1050, 1208, 1277, 1282, 1300, 1339, 1545-1548.

Clausulae
  166, 546, 761, 781, 950, 1215, 1271.

Clavichord music. see Harpsichord music

Compostela school. see Organa; Tropes

Concertos (Violin)
  5, 1580-1583.

Concerti grossi
    Includes excerpts.
  108, 363-364, 720, 1368, 1514-1516, 1584-1586.

Conductus
  160, 340, 404, 437, 718, 1068, 1080, 1112, 1151, 1186, 1214, 1216-1217,
  1261, 1293-1294, 1329, 1552, 1559-1560.

Courantes
  564, 1319.

DANCES

Dances ⌐instrumental⌐
    BALLI: 165, 798. GERMAN: 67, 151, 649, 1095-1097, 1102, 1268.
    HUNGARIAN: 1168. MUSETTE: 1302. NOTA: 1105. POLISH: 760, 1102,
    1247-1248. SPANISH: 1607. TROTTO: 1529. OTHER: 619, 1301, 1304.
        see also Allemandes; Basses danses; Branles; Courantes;
        Ductia; Estampies; Galliards; Gavottes; Gigues;
        Hornpipes; Minuets; Passamezzi, Pavanes; Polonaises;
        Saltarelli; Sarabandes; Suites

Discant, English. see Fauxbourdon

Ductia
    459-460.

Estampies
    515-524.

Fantasias (Harpsichord ⌐piano⌐)
    99, 143, 1492.

Fantasias (Instrumental ensemble)
    147, 245, 417, 956, 1279, 1613.

Fantasias (Lute)
    81, 444, 526, 552, 837, 1029, 1616.

Fantasias (Organ)
    1475-1477.

Fantasias (Violin)
    1493.

Fauxbourdon
    75, 161, 192-193, 465, 468, 470, 551, 655, 684, 795, 831, 1101, 1359.

Frottole
    26, 39, 71-72, 154, 205-206, 213, 214, 286-290, 406, 419-420, 926, 1223,
    1427, 1459, 1524-1527, 1633.

Fugues: see also Canons, and 258 (Tiento)

Fugues (Harpsichord)
    139-142, 144, 863, 1160, 1306.

Fugues (Instrumental ensemble)
    115, 1132, 1399.

Fugues (Organ)
    105, 111, 132-133, 239-241, 256, 543-544, 679, 928, 1387, 1532.

Fugues, Vocal
    672.

Galliards
    74, 246, 604, 606, 626, 759, 977, 1065, 1192, 1232, 1403, 1474.

Gavottes
    1076, 1296.

Gigues
    331, 873, 1319, 1601.

Gymel. see Fauxbourdon

120

Harpsichord music
    Includes piano and "keyboard".
    73, 98, 378, 380-383, 1078, 1234-1235, 1245, 1303, 1305.
        see also Canzoni; Dances; Fantasias; Fugues; Preludes;
            Sonatas (Keyboard); Suites; Variations

Hockets
    790, 792-793, 827.

Hornpipes
    89.

Hymns
    65, 192-193, 401, 464-465, 468-470, 481-482, 1088, 1466.
        see also Chants; Chorales

Instrumental ensembles
    149, 277, 338, 542, 637, 648, 651, 779, 816, 870, 1167, 1315, 1494,
    1512.
        see also Canzoni; Concertos; Dances; Fantasias; Fugues;
            Intradas; Motets; Overtures; Ricercari, Sonatas;
            Suites; Trio-sonatas; Variations

Intonazioni (Organ)
    313, 585-586, 595.
        see also Preludes (Organ)

Intradas
    756, 1230.

Jeu-parti. see Trouvère songs

Lais ⌐Trouvère⌐
    194, 498, 695, 711.

Laisses. see Trouvère songs

Laude
    4, 77-78, 96, 547, 653-654, 682, 799, 830, 922, 1148, 1360, 1554, 1558.

Lieder. see Meisterlieder; Minnelieder; Part-songs, Secular, German;
            Songs, Secular, German

Liturgical dramas
    402, 767, 789, 796, 1004, 1151.

Lute music
    73, 285, 451, 618, 620-621, 1094, 1131, 1225, 1450.
        see also Dances; Fantasias; Preludes; Ricercari; Toccatas; Variations

Madrigals, English
    172, 251, 452, 638, 673, 1062-1064, 1611.

Madrigals, Italian
    EARLY RENAISSANCE: JACOPO: 815, 817-819. LANDINI: 891-893, 896, 898.
    OTHER: 494, 645-646, 959.
    LATE RENAISSANCE: ARCADELT: 82, 84-86. GESUALDO: 627-632.
    MARENZIO: 986-989. MONTEVERDI: 1045-1048, 1056. OTHER: 150, 270,
    533-534, 912, 972, 974, 1170, 1182, 1331-1333, 1426, 1557, 1617.
        see also Songs, Secular, Italian

Magnificats
     189, 978, 1060, 1587.
          For organ settings, see Organ music

Masses
          Other than chant (for which, see Chants)
          Includes excerpts and isolated movements.
     14th CENT.: 655, 700-702, 1002, 1035-1036, 1194, 1359.
     15th CENT.: DEPRÈS: 423-429. DUFAY: 472, 474-479. LA RUE: 903-906.
     OCKEGHEM: 1137-1143. OTHER: 164, 185, 221, 341-342, 386, 485, 490,
     536, 539, 670, 811-812, 937, 1003, 1122, 1154, 1257, 1259-1260, 1273.
     16th CENT.: PALESTRINA: 1174-1181. OTHER: 346, 660, 913, 971, 1040,
     1070, 1272, 1363, 1490, 1569.
     18th CENT.: 116-117, 584, 749, 1374.

Masses (Organ)
          Includes excerpts and isolated movements.
     222, 257, 315-316, 395, 561, 881, 928, 1033.

Meisterlieder ₍15th-16th cent.₎
     548, 1345-1350.

Minnelieder ₍ca.1150-1318₎
     92, 178, 557-559, 856, 874, 982, 1089-1093, 1342, 1449, 1485,
     1602-1604, 1628-1631.

Minuets
     357, 385, 1076-1077, 1084.

Motets
     13th CENT.: 49, 94, 160, 282, 333, 344, 409, 445-446, 499, 525, 781
     783, 786, 791, 793, 825, 827, 957, 994, 1037, 1067, 1071, 1117, 1149,
     1270-1271, 1287, 1289-1290, 1355, 1519, 1528.
     14th CENT.: 60, 272, 529-530, 692, 704, 709-710, 782, 1224.
     15th CENT.: DEPRÈS: 413, 430, 433-434. DUNSTABLE: 483-484, 488-489, 491.
     ISAAC: 804-805, 808, 813. OBRECHT: 1120, 1123-1125. OTHER: 80, 223,
     351, 462-463, 535, 579, 1072, 1255-1256, 1258, 1286, 1509, 1614-1615.
     16th CENT.: BRUCK: 218-220. G GABRIELI: 594, 596-598. HANDL: 743-746.
     LASSUS: 907, 909, 911, 914, 919. PALESTRINA: 1169, 1171-1173, 1183.
     SENFL: 1430, 1432, 1441. TALLIS: 1481-1483. VICTORIA: 1568, 1570-1572.
     WILLAERT: 1620-1622, 1626. OTHER: 30, 247-248, 349, 458, 513, 589,
     661-662, 680, 750-751, 764, 797, 847, 852, 869, 925, 927, 931, 947,
     979-980, 1059, 1061, 1086, 1153, 1318, 1364, 1595, 1598.
     LATE 16th-18th CENT.: 279, 334, 384, 833, 1057, 1263, 1265, 1408, 1498,
     1567, 1591.
          see also Motets, Isorhythmic

Motets (Instrumental ensemble)
     790, 792-794, 1146.

Motets, Isorhythmic
     64, 171, 492, 531, 622, 705, 1116, 1233.

Notre Dame school ₍ca.1150-1250₎ see Clausulae; Conductus; Motets; Organa;
                                        and LEONINUS and PEROTINUS in Part 1

Operas - Excerpts
     303, 305, 1207.
          For single excerpts, see Arias; Choruses; Overtures;
          Recitatives; and 148, 327, 1208.

Oratorios - Excerpts
    293, 1413-1415, 1418.
        For single excerpts, see Arias; Choruses; Overtures; Recitatives

Organ music
    254, 258-260, 312, 350, 778, 976, 1189-1190, 1311-1312, 1400-1401, 1511.
        see also Canzoni; Chorale preludes; Dances; Fantasias; Fugues;
                Harpsichord music; Intonazioni; Masses (Organ);
                Preludes; Ricercari; Toccatas; Variations

Organa
    24, 37, 54, 57-59, 62, 168-170, 355-356, 398-399, 405, 436, 681, 762-763,
    772, 949, 951, 1031, 1066, 1083, 1213, 1218, 1321, 1404, 1465, 1530,
    1538, 1542, 1555, 1573.

Oriental music ⌐ancient⌐
    508, 582.

Overtures
        Includes excerpts from large works.
    179, 275, 328, 729, 732, 884, 963, 966, 970, 1184, 1238, 1275, 1335,
    1361, 1367, 1370, 1373, 1376-1377, 1463, 1608.
        see also Intradas; Preludes

Part-songs, Sacred
    197, 495, 717, 902, 1464, 1539, 1599.
        see also Anthems; Carols; Chorales; Choruses, Sacred;
                Clausulae; Conductus; Fauxbourdon; Hymns; Laude;
                Motets; Organa; Psalms; Tropes

Part-songs, Secular ⌐by language⌐: for 2 or more solo voices; for larger
                                    groups, see Choruses, Secular

Part-songs, Secular, English
    152-153, 359, 373-374, 454, 456, 497, 771, 1113, 1241, 1486, 1610, 1612.
        see also Canons; Fauxbourdon; Madrigals

Part-songs, Secular, Flemish
    1025.

Part-songs, Secular, French.   see Ballades; Canons; Chansons, Polyphonic;
                                    Chansons mesurées; Hockets; Rondeaux;
                                    Virelais

Part-songs, Secular, German
    HASSLER: 753-755, 757.   HOFHAIMER: 774-777.   ISAAC: 801, 809, 814.
    SENFL: 1431, 1434-1439, 1443.   OTHER: 91, 217, 408, 512, 538, 554, 556,
    647, 677, 910, 946, 948, 1340, 1366, 1395, 1398, 1454, 1579, 1590, 1618.
        see also Quodlibets; Villanelle

Part-songs, Secular, Italian
    73, 432, 493, 807, 1128, 1152, 1199.
        see also Ballate; Balletti; Canons; Frottole;
                Madrigals; Quodlibets; Villanelle

Part-songs, Secular, Latin
    1023, 1440, 1523.
        see also Canons; Fauxbourdon; Quodlibets

Part-songs, Secular, Spanish.   see Villancicos

PASSACAGLIAS

Passacaglias. see Variations

Passamezzi
   68, 1187.

Passions. see Oratorios

Pastourelles ⌐Troubadour, Trouvère¬
   2, 12, 90, 93.

Pavanes
   226, 626, 635, 640, 759, 1065, 1191-1192, 1232, 1254, 1393, 1472, 1474.

Polonaises
   145, 849.

Preludes: includes excerpts from suites, etc.
      see also Intradas; Overtures

Preludes (Harpsichord)
   134, 139-140, 142, 227, 737, 1079.

Preludes (Lute)
   1098, 1320.

Preludes (Organ)
   105, 133, 230-231, 239-240, 543-544, 787, 850-851, 854, 1188, 1386-1387,
   1532.
      see also Intonazioni

Psalms
   207-208, 347-348, 527, 589, 663-669, 870, 915-916, 941, 1172, 1345,
   1416-1417, 1467, 1478, 1482, 1591.
      see also Chants

Quodlibets
   541, 555, 570, 650, 806, 1402.

Recitatives
      Includes excerpts from large works.
   CARISSIMI: 293, 295-297. CAVALLI: 308-311. HÄNDEL: 730, 733, 738.
   LULLY: 961-962, 965. MONTEVERDI: 1043, 1049, 1051, 1054.
   RAMEAU: 1297-1299. SCHÜTZ: 1409, 1413-1415, 1418-1419.
   OTHER: 119-120, 274, 281, 304, 306, 335-336, 457, 603, 747, 844,
   985, 1009, 1200, 1202, 1209, 1212, 1276, 1281, 1369, 1500.

Requiems. see Masses

Ricercari
   256, 317-318, 400, 562, 587, 601, 609, 642, 864, 1014, 1451-1452,
   1623-1624.

Rondeaux ⌐vocal¬
   12th CENT.: 340. 13th CENT. (Trouvère): 14, 16-18, 66, 70, 252,
   688-689, 1220. 14th CENT.: 698, 708.
   15th CENT.: 186, 190-191, 353, 360-362, 461, 466, 899, 901, 1005, 1069.

Rotrouenges ⌐Trouvère¬
   337, 687, 713, 1324-1325.

Rounds. see Canons

Saint Martial school ⌐10th cent.-1150¬ see Organa; Tropes

Saltarelli
   204, 1352-1354, 1473.

Sarabandes
   332, 1077, 1319, 1601.

Sequences ⌈liturgical⌉
   19, 52, 442, 838, 1083, 1106-1107, 1109-1111, 1553, 1555, 1627.

Sinfonie. see Overtures

Sonatas (Instrumental ensemble)
   38, 599, 939, 1229.

Sonatas (Keyboard)
   100-104, 871-872, 1243-1244, 1343, 1380-1385.

Sonatas (Solo with continuo)
   180-183, 319, 365-366, 549-550, 571, 736, 933-934, 995-996, 998,
   1344, 1447, 1455, 1487-1489.

Sonatas (2 instruments with continuo) see Trio-sonatas

Songs, Greek ⌈ancient⌉
   840, 1020-1022, 1242, 1428.
      see also Chants, Greek

Songs, Sacred
   10th CENT.: 1448. 12th CENT.: 656-658. 13th CENT.: 43, 46, 1115.
   14th CENT.: 992, 1250. 17th CENT.: 31, 350, 384, 391, 741, 1334,
   1336, 1423, 1563-1566. 18th CENT.: 97, 198, 1499.
      see also Hymns; Laude; Part-songs, Sacred;
           Psalms; Villancicos; Virelais

Songs, Secular ⌈by language⌉: for single voice; for 2 or more voices,
                      see Part-songs, Secular

      see also Arias

Songs, Secular, Czech
   868.

Songs, Secular, English
   224, 278, 403, 453, 455-456, 800, 981, 1337, 1632.

Songs, Secular, French
   163, 209-210, 388, 443, 780, 1104.
      see also Ballades; Chansons, Polyphonic; Chansons mesurées;
           Troubadour songs; Trouvère songs; Virelais

Songs, Secular, German
   15th CENT.: 540, 954-955, 993, 1561. 16th CENT.: 1442.
   17th CENT.: 32-36, 675, 742, 848, 858-862, 865, 1410.
   18th CENT.: 122, 572, 659, 1084, 1405, 1458, 1496.
      see also Meisterlieder; Minnelieder

Songs, Secular, Hungarian
   1510.

Songs, Secular, Italian
   262-268, 301, 375, 973, 1461.
      see also Frottole

Songs, Secular, Latin
    11th CENT.: 766, 1118.

Songs, Secular, Spanish
    8, 580-581, 1026.
        see also Villancicos

Stantipes. see Estampies

Suites: for excerpted movements, see list of headings under Dances;
        Preludes (Harpsichord); and 542, 956, 1320, 1335.

Suites (Harpsichord)
    76, 131, 135, 545, 573, 575-576, 1162-1163, 1285.

Suites (Instrumental ensemble)
    1226-1228, 1266, 1394, 1469, 1575.

Suites (Orchestra)
    136.

Symphonies
        Includes excerpts.
    276, 1039, 1357, 1456.

Toccatas
    241, 553, 563, 568-569, 577, 591, 1015-1019, 1164.

Trio-sonatas
    6, 367-372, 739, 940, 1011, 1206, 1306, 1309, 1356, 1457, 1517,
    1576-1578.

Tropes
    24, 37, 170, 396-397, 399, 578, 882-883, 935, 1001, 1321, 1323, 1465,
    1534-1535.

Troubadour songs
    174, 176, 716, 983, 1288, 1295.
        see also Albas; Ballades; Cansos; Pastourelles; Vers

Trouvère songs
    11, 13, 712, 714, 1038 (sequence), 1328, 1504 (jeu-parti), 1506, 1508,
    1549 (strophic laisse).
        see also Albas; Ballades; Lais; Pastourelles;
                Rondeaux; Rotrouenges; Vers; Virelais

Trumpet music
    159.

Variations (Harpsichord)
    68, 89, 228, 243-244, 255, 330, 528, 565, 1081, 1085, 1237, 1246, 1284,
    1316, 1520.

Variations (Instrumental ensemble)
    183, 280, 969, 997, 1187, 1226.

Variations (Lute)
    158, 354, 1087, 1544.

Variations (Organ)
    132, 253, 929, 1075, 1388-1389, 1391-1392, 1600.

Vers
    TROUBADOUR: 175, 615, 984, 1193. TROUVÈRE: 1221, 1505, 1522.

Vers mesurés. see Chansons mesurées

Vihuela music. see Lute music

Villancicos
    40, 42, 44-45, 320, 500-506, 1027-1028, 1030, 1253.

Villanelle; Villanesche
    345, 448-449, 932, 990-991, 1103, 1313-1314, 1362, 1365, 1619.

Violin music. see Concertos; Fantasias; Sonatas (Solo with continuo);
                Trio-sonatas

Virelais
    TROUVÈRE: 10, 685-686, 826, 1150. 13th CENT.: 41, 47-48.
    14th CENT.: 343, 690-691, 694, 703, 707, 1543.
    15th CENT.: 473, 1135-1136.
        see also Laude

Virginals music. see Harpsichord music